OPEN THE FRONTIERS

Léon Joseph Cardinal Suenens

OPEN THE FRONTIERS

Conversations with CARDINAL SUENENS

Foreword by Helder Camara

Interviewed by Karl-Heinz Fleckenstein
Translated by Olga Prendergast

THE SEABURY PRESS · New York

1981
The Seabury Press
815 Second Avenue
New York, N.Y. 10017

Translation copyright © 1980 by Darton, Longman and Todd Ltd.

Originally published in German as *Fuer die Kirche von Morgen* and
copyright © 1979 by Neue Stadt-Verlag Muenchen. This English
translation was made by Olga Prendergast from the French edition
published by Nouvelle Cite, Paris.

Printed in the United States of America

Library of Congress Cataloging in Publication Data

Suenens, Léon Joseph, Cardinal, 1904–
Open the frontiers.
Translation of Für die Kirche von Morgen.
1. Catholic Church—Doctrinal and controversial works
—Catholic authors. I. Fleckenstein, Karl-Heinz.
II. Title.
BX1751.2.S8313   1981   230'.2   80-39629
ISBN 0-8164-0489-5

Contents

Acknowledgements

Biblical quotations are in general from the Jerusalem Bible, © 1966, 1967 and 1968 Darton, Longman & Todd Ltd and Doubleday and Company, Inc.

Vatican II documents are taken from *Documents of Vatican II* (edited by Walter M. Abbott, SJ) London, Geoffrey Chapman, 1966.

The translated extract of *Evangelii Nuntiandi* is reproduced by kind permission of The Incorporated Catholic Truth Society, London.

'Open the frontiers of states to his saving power, open the economic systems and the political systems, the vast realms of culture, civilization and development. Do not be afraid!'

Pope John Paul II

FOREWORD

This new book, *Open the Frontiers*, is a beautiful and timely present from Cardinal Suenens for bishops, priests, lay people, non-Christians and non-believers alike.

The questions raised are thought-provoking. What do we think of the distinction between democracy and co-responsibility? Do we agree that, ideally, a bishop should think 'right' and feel 'left'? Is it by chance that the Creator made us with a right half and a left half, but took care to place our heart on the left?

Suenens was probably the greatest of the Vatican II Moderators, and without him (for the Lord uses men), the Council may well have taken a different course.

Suenens, who so loves the Holy Spirit and is loved by him, has received above all the gift of demonstrating that, in the final analysis, the love of God and the love of mankind are one and the same great love.

With remarkable skill, Suenens helps us to understand the signs of the times and furthers our dialogue with the world. We have to meditate on what he says about ecumenism and the Third World. Christians of all confessions and people of good will (even if they consider themselves non-believers) will soon discover in this book wonderful suggestions for preparing the advent of the third millennium of the birth of Christ, whose steps on the road of time we can already discern quite clearly.

What I particularly like in these conversations is Suenens's faithful love of the one whom the Father desired to be not only the mother of Christ and the mother of men, but also the exemplary hearer and doer of the Lord's word.

+ Helder Camara,
  Archevêque d' Olinda et Recife (Brésil)
  Paris, le 8 Décembre 1979

PREFACE

Those of us who followed the courageous interventions of Cardinal Suenens as moderator at Vatican II felt that this man was leaving his mark on an important period in the history of the Church. His writing and his speaking reveal a man whose vision of the Church and the world transcends the present. During his remarkable address on "Sport and Religion", given on the occasion of the 1972 Olympics in Munich, I saw in him a kind of passion for mankind. Listening to his farewell oration at the funeral of his friend Cardinal Döpfner, I felt him to be a man of the Church who always obeys the promptings of the Holy Spirit, wherever they may be manifested. And during an ecumenical meeting at Augsburg, I saw him as a pastor who has set his heart on Christian unity, as a man at once contemplative and active, always ready to learn and to pass on what he has learned.

In the course of the long and unforgettable conversation I had with him at his residence in Malines, I endeavoured to discover the golden thread that runs through his life and work. In evoking his memories the Cardinal never placed himself apart from others, but always integrated himself into the vast network of human relationships. Nor would he consider men *en masse,* for he regarded each man as a person who deserves full attention and to whom no sweeping generalization is applicable.

In the first part of this book, it was not just the Cardinal's words which revealed to me this great charismatic figure of our time; rather it was his barely perceptible gestures, his chiselled features, reminiscent of the profile of Roman senators; his high forehead, his deep eyes, so kindly and smiling, which seem to read the very soul of his interlocutor; the great sensitiveness with which he listens to others; his disarming humour.

In the second part of the book, where our conversations were held mainly in writing, I was time and again astonished by his exceptional intellectual ability to grasp situations and problems in their right proportions and to avoid extremes. At the same time, I was discovering the simple faith of a child in this man who regards the world as his parish. It was in this friendly atmosphere that the following conversations took place.

Karl-Heinz Fleckenstein

PART ONE

1

A Priest with a Vision
of the Universal Church

*Cardinal, the 'golden thread' which guides your life is not un-
related to your episcopal motto,* 'in spiritu sancto ex maria
virgine'*: by the Holy Spirit from the Virgin Mary.*

Yes, the Holy Spirit has always held a special place in
my life. I've sought to give him absolute priority. My
episcopal motto also highlights Mary: Christ was born
of the Spirit and of Mary. And this mystery is perpetu-
ated in the Church. It's thanks to Mary's *fiat* that Christ
gives himself to the world throughout the ages. I see
Mary as the one who lets herself be filled to overflowing
by the Holy Spirit and who thus receives the unique gift
of the Motherhood of God. For me, she expresses, as the
first charismatic of the Church, complete receptiveness,
complete self-giving. She plays no role on the institutional plane, but she belongs to the plane of spiritual
readiness and draws us to it with her.

*Were you able to discover the Holy Spirit's action and Mary's
hidden presence even as a child?*

The fact that I was born on 16 July, the feast of Our
Lady of Carmel, that my first school was run by the
Marists, that the Archiepiscopal College of Schaerbeek
was called 'Sainte Marie' – today I regard all these
things as an affectionate smile from Mary.

3

It was on the death of my father, I believe, that I first experienced the action of the Holy Spirit. I was only four at the time. His premature death made me understand how short and frail our existence is. I look upon this as a grace. After my father's death, my mother was left with only a small income. This hidden poverty, which is also a grace, made a lasting impression on me. As a child, I had no books of my own, not even school books. We just couldn't afford them. On the other hand, I was given a lifelong, priceless treasure: my mother's simple and profound piety. Her trust in providence, her selflessness and courage have enriched my whole life. Morally she was, like Mary at the foot of the cross, a woman of great strength who could bear suffering and want, the hardships of the war and, later, her illness, with patience and trust. Still later, during the years when I studied philosophy and theology, she made many sacrifices for my sake. When I had to decide whether I would study in Belgium or in Rome at the Gregorian, she said to me, 'Make your decision before God, without taking account of me.' So her life was for me an education in Christianity, lived in self-forgetfulness. By the example of her life, she helped me to discover the meaning of the priesthood.

Were there any others who played an important role in your choice of the priesthood?

Indirectly my uncle, Father E. Janssen, who had baptized me. My mother and I lived with him for a year. I think that the fact of having lived in close proximity with a priest opened me to the prospect of the priesthood. I began to understand more clearly how short life is, and also the ephemeral nature of everything that isn't eternal. So I decided to orientate my life in relation to eternity. My own life and my neighbour's, for I wanted

4

to reveal the secret of happiness for this world and the hereafter to my neighbour as well.

Cardinal, your seven years of study in Rome were a stage towards your priesthood, a time spent at the very centre of the universal Church. Did this affect you in any way?

Yes, it was there that I discovered very concretely the meaning of the words of the Creed: 'I believe in one holy catholic and apostolic Church.' We had the 'one' Church constantly before our eyes. We were living that unity as a tangible reality. We were living the unity, the catholicity of the Church, and also its apostolicity, close to the tombs of the apostles Peter and Paul. We were encountering the universal Church in our daily contact with our fellow students, of all races and languages. All these things steep you in the life of the Church.

The 'Eternal City' exists not only in relation to its past. I imagine that the personalities who live there also contribute to its atmosphere. Would you agree?

Yes, and there were quite a few in my student days. People like the Benedictine monk Dom Lambert Beauduin, then Professor of Theology at San Anselmo. Dom Lambert subsequently founded the ecumenical monastery of Chevetogne, which is still an important centre for Christian rapprochement. During our long and unforgettable conversations in Rome, he initiated me into the thought of the Greek Fathers; he opened up trinitarian horizons for me and awakened in my soul a love of the Holy Spirit. It was he who drafted the famous memorandum which Cardinal Mercier read on the occasion of the Malines Conversations: *The Anglican Church, United but not Absorbed*. Dom Lambert always remained faithful to his aim of bringing Orthodox, Anglicans and Catholics closer to one another. Cardinal Angelo Roncalli, at the time Patriarch of Venice, once congratulated him on his prophetic vision and his method. The idea of convoking a Council had already been suggested to the future Pope by Dom Lambert Beauduin in the course of their conversations.

Another figure encountered in Rome who made a deep impression on me was Father Vincent Lebbe. He had consecrated his life to the apostolate in China: he really lived as a Chinese among the Chinese. He spoke, wrote, thought and dressed like a Chinese. The care of Chinese students in Europe was his special concern. He used to travel through Belgium, France and Switzerland looking for schools and colleges for them, or for Catholic families who would welcome them. His efforts were rewarded when at last he had the joy of attending the nomination of the first six Chinese bishops by Pius XI in Rome. 'The real missionary problem', he once explained to me during a private conversation we held for seven hours, 'is that, if the Church wants to preach the Gospel effectively, it must be Chinese in China, Indian in India, and so on. It cannot be an exclusively Latin or European Church.' This vision of true catholicity made an indelible impression on me; and more, I felt that Father Lebbe's views confirmed those of Dom Lambert who, in another connection, had awakened my interest in Eastern Christians and Anglicans, and my sympathy for them. All these inspirations were converging and opening up new horizons for me.

Did you also see the weaknesses, the petty side of Rome in those days?

Obviously, I was in a position to realize that, wherever men exist, you find weaknesses and pettiness. But this didn't affect my faith in God and my deep love of the

Church. I would say to myself, 'human beings are relative, only God is absolute. We all carry our treasures in fragile vessels.' The grace of God would immunize me against the temptation to confuse the essential with the secondary, the lasting with the incidental, the positiveness of the divine with the negativeness of the human. This grace would also help me to retain that indispensable dash of Christian humour. I would often think of John of the Cross, who calls the appearance of things 'il pintado', the painted facade, and urges us to penetrate their visible aspect with the eyes of the spirit. Although there was as yet no John XXIII to throw open the windows of the Church with the *aggiornamento* and let in the fresh air, I was already convinced of the necessity of a renewal.

So you do feel that participation in this renewal of the Church is essential to your vocation?

That concern for its revitalization has remained with me until this day like a constant spur. When I entered the Belgian College in Rome, I hoped to find a spiritual life there. But I didn't find it. Even the lectures at the Gregorian were disappointing: the philosophy was too scholastic, too abstract, not integrated with life. All serious confrontation with modern tendencies of thought was avoided. The theology proved too speculative, too apologetical. But my hope for the revitalization of the Church never deserted me, for only a renewed Church can accomplish the renewal of the world. And this remains my profound conviction. Impelled by that conviction, I put my trust in the logic of faith. This, too, I regard as a special gift of the Holy Spirit. For at the same time I was becoming mindful of many human failings and, hence, of the relativeness of all human activity. I would often think of Cardinal Newman's say-

7

ing: 'Ten thousand difficulties do not make one doubt.'
The divine mystery of the Church transcends all sociological dimensions.

*Wasn't your encounter with your great predecessor Cardinal Mer-
cier a turning-point in your life?*

I'll never forget that encounter at the end of the summer
of 1921. I was seventeen when I first met the Cardinal,
who was already in his seventies. In the years that followed, Mercier increasingly became what I would call
my spiritual father. It was thanks to his initiative that
I was able to study at the Pontifical University in Rome.
During the holidays his secretary, Canon Dessain, would
often invite me to his home and tell me many details
concerning the Cardinal's life and activities. On each
occasion I realized with astonishment how far ahead of
his time this great churchman was: in his all-embracing
view of the world, his openness, his kindness, his level-
headedness and serenity, his understanding of human
problems. He was a man who lived by the profound
conviction that the Holy Spirit works constantly in each
individual as much as in the whole Church. When he
celebrated his priestly jubilee, he revealed the secret of
his success:

> Every day put your work aside for five minutes. Iso-
> late yourself from the world of the senses; close your
> ears to the surrounding noises, retire into the sanc-
> tuary of your soul, which through baptism has become
> the temple of the Holy Spirit. Then say this: 'Holy
> Spirit, soul of my soul, I worship you. Enlighten me,
> guide me, strengthen and comfort me! Tell me what
> I must do and command me to do it! I promise to be
> obedient whatever you may desire of me, to accept

everything that happens to me by your will. Only show me what you want of me!'

'If you do this,' he used to say, 'complete comfort will be yours, even in moments of affliction.'

When Cardinal Mercier came to Rome for the election of Pope Pius XI, he gave me a copy of his book *A mes séminaristes*. One day I asked him to give me a motto which would help me to prepare for the priesthood. He replied, 'Strive to renounce everything that is not God himself. He alone suffices.' He had himself practised this way of life. Pastoral work remained his chief preoccupation. During the First World War he was, as it were, a voice of conscience for the Belgian people: he brought them support and firm confidence, he spoke fearlessly to the occupying power.

Wasn't he also a great ecumenist in his day?

In addition to his concern for his seminarians at Malines and his interest in philosophical questions, his breadth of vision was revealed mainly in the famous Malines Conversations, which he held with Lord Halifax and a group of Anglican theologians from 1921 to 1926. The aim was to find a common area of reconciliation for the Roman Catholic Church and the Anglican Communion. I was still a student then, and I used to follow with great interest the ecumenical discussions of those men who were so full of faith and courage. For me, they opened up new prospects of Christian unity. They helped me to love the Church as it was. They helped me to understand that the Church is as vast as the world, that it transcends all cultures, that the restoration of visible unity among Christians remained an imperative, and that it was worthwhile devoting one's life to it till one's dying breath.

How many times were these Malines Conversations held?

In all there were about five meetings, which were discontinued because of Cardinal Mercier's death. On his deathbed he offered his episcopal ring to Lord Halifax as a symbol of friendship and a sign of hope. This ring was later set in a chalice which is now in York Minster.

In their time the Malines Conversations were a bold undertaking. Of course, they had quite a few critics, but a characteristic of all prophetic action, it seems, is that some time has to elapse before its meaning becomes clear. It was in this light that, many years later, I read Paul VI's message to the Anglican Church on the occasion of the canonization of the forty English Martyrs:

> There will be no seeking to lessen the legitimate prestige and the worthy patrimony of piety and usage proper to the Anglican Church when the Roman Catholic Church – this humble 'servant of the servants of God' – is able to embrace her beloved sister in the one authentic communion of the family of Christ: a communion of origin and of faith, a communion of priesthood and of rule, a communion of the saints in the freedom and love of the Spirit of Christ.

Did the Malines Conversations usher you, as it were, into the ecumenical movement?

In a way, yes. For, from that moment, one idea remained with me permanently: all Christians must advance towards unity, individually and jointly, with respect for their own traditions on the plane of liturgy, canon law and the like, but adhering to one and the same faith. Because as long as we Christians remain disunited, the world cannot have faith. Unity does not mean uniformity at all levels. The Church once again visibly united became the great dream of my life.

10

Then you were ordained priest at Malines by Mercier's successor, Cardinal van Roey?

That was an unforgettable moment. During the celebration we prostrated ourselves on the paving of the Cathedral as a symbolic gesture of self-surrender and humility before God; we prayed to the Lord to accept our lives, to help us to become his witnesses and to spread the mystery of God faithfully. At the moment when we promised respect and obedience to the bishop, I was thinking of Jesus' words to Peter, 'Another will gird you and carry you where you do not wish to go' (John 21:18). From that moment I considered that my personal life had become permanently identified with fidelity to the Church's tasks, with which I would be entrusted.

Then you returned to Rome?

Yes, I still had two more years of study and I had to take my doctorate in theology. This was a very rich period in my life, for I was becoming more and more interested in the problems of the Church in its relation to the world. That's why I undertook, with my bishop's consent, to serve as correspondent for *La Métropole*, a Belgian paper with liberal tendencies. I would read five or six papers a day and, in this way, I kept in touch with what was happening in the world at the time. Writing under the pseudonym of Testis, I would report events like the Lateran Agreements, the March on Rome, in short all the topical news from Italy.

When did you return to your diocese?

In September 1929. Then Cardinal van Roey sent me to my old college *Sainte Marie* as a lower secondary teacher. I was just down from university and it wasn't very easy for me to adjust to the mentality of twelve-year-olds. And yet, from a spiritual point of view, I look back on that period as a time of great grace. Teaching children to write, helping them with their prep, teaching them grammar and French, all those simple things were helping me to cast off the burden of intellectualism. From then on I was to be a priest, no more and no less, ready to render the service that would be expected of me for the rest of my life. Hadn't I promised obedience to my bishop after all?

And for how long did you teach those children to write?

Six months. Then I was appointed professor of philosophy at the Seminary of Malines. Obviously, this needed far less self-adjustment. Over the next ten years my work consisted in teaching future priests philosophy, ethics, history and pedagogy. It was an opportunity to give the students a much broader training, ranging far beyond purely scholastic thinking. Apart from my classes, when I conducted a preaching mission or a retreat, I would lay special emphasis on the significance of the Risen Christ, on the significance of both the Passover event and the experience of the power of the Holy Spirit as the vivifier of every life and every religious action. It was only later, after I was nominated bishop, that I understood the importance of those years, for quite a few priests of my diocese were old pupils of mine. And this greatly facilitated our contacts in the pastoral field.

2

A Bishop Alive to Doctrine
and to its Vital Repercussions

*From 1940 to 1945 you were Vice-Rector of the University of
Louvain; then on 16 December 1945 you became Auxiliary Bishop
to Cardinal van Roey. Looking back on that new function, what
did you feel about it at the time?*

In those days I was entrusted with tasks which I would
never have chosen for myself. My work as Auxiliary
Bishop was concerned far more with fulfilling functions
than with assuming responsibilities. For example, I had
to administer confirmation, grant imprimaturs, and also
perform a kind of supervisory function in church administration. I devoted my free time to various research
studies and also to promoting the Legion of Mary as an
instrument for the lay apostolate.

*Many of your opinions and ideas stem from that period, but at
the time they seemed almost too revolutionary.*

Probably because the time wasn't ripe. Today, with the
benefit of hindsight, I would say that, in my own life,
that period of preparation, reflection and meditation on
the renewal of the Church was, as it were, the sowing of
what subsequently germinated during the Council.

When, on 16 November 1961, you succeeded Cardinal van Roey,

13

you said in your pastoral message that, as a successor of the apostles, a bishop must show forth Christ in every sphere of life, but that he can't fulfil this task without the co-operation and willing support of others. Didn't those words on coresponsibility announce the direction you intended to give your whole episcopate?

Yes, indeed. From that day my desire has always been to make room in my diocese for greater coresponsibility, for the formation of a more collegial community. All my interventions must be interpreted in this light. This doesn't mean that the Church should be envisaged as a democracy in which a majority dictates the law to a minority. Yet one mustn't be afraid of the free expression of opinions, or even of confrontation, should it prove necessary.

Every Friday from 10 a.m. to 4 p.m. I consult with seventeen of my closest co-workers and we hold a collegial discussion. I think that, over the last fifteen years, I've taken, at the very most, only three or four decisions which conflicted with their common view.

Besides, team work is essential in countless social tasks, such as an Apollo space project, medical research, the effective treatment of leukemia, problems of military, scientific or social organization, and so on. The task of decision makers has become so complex that they must increasingly act as good co-ordinators, like the conductor leading his orchestra. Men are becoming more and more aware of the value of joint effort and, as a wise man pointed out, they have to put their heads together to be intelligent. In the life of the Church, we too have to rely on that discernment. Coresponsibility means that each member co-operates in the common good, freely and with due respect for others.

Although the Church has largely contributed to the earthly happiness of mankind, it is primarily a spiritual reality, rooted in eternity. The Church isn't just a spiri-

14

tual 'Red Cross'. It speaks to its contemporaries, it lives in a ceaselessly developing world. That's why theology and pastoral practice have to be constantly adapted to changing circumstances, but without diminishing the revealed truth. The Church needs capable Christians in every area: administration, jurisprudence, education, culture. . . . It needs the talent of writers and the perspicacity of sociologists. In the sphere of family and marriage problems, it needs the knowledge of doctors, psychologists and psychiatrists. So today a wide-ranging application of the principle of apostolic coresponsibility is more essential than ever.

For thirty years or so you've held a teaching function in the Church. What importance do you attach to the gift of discerning spirits?

My main task – I venture to say my principal duty as a bishop – is to consider everything in the light of faith, and therefore to state clearly what faith ultimately signifies for man. Consequently, it's important to distinguish the Christian faith from less permanent things determined by our culture. We must constantly distinguish between the essential and the unessential.

Today people tend to make a facile distinction between 'religious' Christians and 'socially committed' Christians. To which category would you say you belong?

Recently Dom Helder Camara and I wrote a book entitled *Charismatic Renewal and Social Action* in order to demonstrate how inseparably united these two aspects are. We Christians have to show how perfectly they harmonize. For the Holy Spirit, acting in us, guarantees the genuineness of our relationship with both God and mankind. That's the meaning of the invocation which

15

the Church's liturgy so often places on our lips: 'Send forth thy Spirit, and thou shalt renew the face of the earth.' These words have vast implications and must be meditated in depth: for anyone looking at the face of the earth today feels more inclined to give way to fear and doubt than to renew anything!

Our contemporaries are anxiously asking themselves what will happen to the human race if tomorrow some irresponsible official were, even accidentally, to push the button that could plunge the whole world into an apocalyptic nuclear devastation. What will happen when science discovers how to manipulate man at will, throughout his life, from his first to his last day on earth? How will man react when political power gains exceptionally effective means of influencing the public opinion and conduct of whole populations? That's why today it's more essential than ever for Christians to learn what true freedom is, freedom renewed by the Holy Spirit. They have to open themselves to him in order to cope with the problems that are imperilling human life and our civilization. They have to enter the Upper Room to receive, through prayer, the light and power of his vivifying presence. But then they have to come out of the Upper Room and witness to that presence in the heart of the world, with humble and brotherly assurance.

As a bishop, you're also called to be the spiritual father of your flock. How can you give everyone that fatherly care in such a large diocese?

I often think of what John Paul II said when, during an audience, he spontaneously took a little child in his arms: 'We need many arms to embrace all men!' Or, as the famous Cardinal Archbishop of Milan, St Charles Borromeo, once said: 'A soul is in itself a sufficiently large diocese for a bishop.'

16

My diocese now has a population of about two million. Obviously, a fatherly relationship involving a personal acquaintance with each inhabitant would be impossible. But fatherhood can assume a variety of forms. Vatican Council II and its breakthroughs ushered in a series of new tasks and duties. I try to fulfil them to the best of my ability. It isn't always easy to carry out one's episcopal task both at local level and as a bishop responsible with many others for the welfare of the universal Church. Sometimes priorities conflict and one has to make difficult decisions which aren't immediately comprehensible to others.

And don't you also have to attend to a great deal of administrative work as a bishop?

The administrative side of my work isn't the heaviest of duties. It can often be delegated to others. My co-workers are very competent in this respect. For instance, I don't have to attend to problems of financial administration.

Is there, in your view, an ideal portrait, a prototype, of the bishop?

There is no unique portrait, although one of St Gregory's writings is said to present the perfect model of the bishop. But I don't believe there really is a prototype. Much depends on circumstances and on one's living environment. The bishop's function has so many different aspects! Ideally, the bishop should be the centre of the Christian community, the point around which its unity is crystallized, so that he brings together and unifies the conflicting currents, and overcomes the polarizations of the Church. . . . It isn't easy!

17

So in this light the bishop is always a man of Christian reconciliation?

His role is to strengthen and communicate faith. He must constantly remind us of our duty to be one in Christ. As a successor of the apostles and a member of the apostolic college, working with and under the guidance of the Pope, he's called to lead the people of God forward, and further forward. In order to spread more justice, equality and true love among men, the bishop must strive to be of one heart and one soul with his flock.

He must also be a builder of bridges, who raises men towards God through communal prayer, and communicates the life of the Trinity to them through the sacraments. Men need a genuine and authorized representative, someone who serves as the guarantor of the living tradition, who passes on from one generation to another the whole of the divine Founder's message. They need to find a meeting-point in his person, so that each one may feel closer to his brother in faith through the intermediary of his bishop. Of course, this task exceeds our human strength. That's why the bishop needs the support of the prayer of the faithful more than any other man.

3

A Writer who Never Sidesteps
the Issue

Your numerous books, translated into many languages, have made you one of the best known writers of our time. How do you come to write your books?

My books aren't inspired by a desire to write. They're not mere speculations but pastoral actions.

In 1951 you wrote a theology of the apostolate. What was the aim of that book?

It sprang from my concern to obey the promptings of the Holy Spirit wherever they may be manifested to me. I was made Auxiliary Bishop in 1945 and soon after I became acquainted with the Legion of Mary. It's interesting to note that it was a Communist convert who first drew my attention to that movement. I then established contact with the Legion of Mary in France, where, as you know, it was beginning to develop. I believed – and still believe – that the Legion is a work of God. I wrote that book to help spread the Legion of Mary, which in those days was still fairly unknown in Europe, and to give it a theological foundation. Its members commit themselves to the Holy Spirit, not directly to Mary. I felt that it was important to stress the close relationship between the Holy Spirit and Mary, for their relationship remains important in the life of the Church. That book

19

is also a plea for greater harmony between prayer and apostolic action, between piety and the active dynamics of the Christian life. So I was also inviting my readers to serve the Lord with imagination, a practical sense and courage.

At the World Health Congress, held in Brussels in 1958, you urged an audience of three thousand members of the medical profession to find a convincing Christian answer to the problem of birth-control. I believe that your book Love and Control *sprang from the findings of the Congress.*

Yes, indeed. I wanted to seize that opportunity to approach one of the most difficult problems of Catholic morality with international experts. I said to my audience:

> You are striving to combat every illness. This is important. But there are also some very critical medical and moral problems. Help us to solve them. We have no right to ask people to keep the law of the Church unless, at the same time, we do everything in our power to make this obedience possible. There are sins of intertia and intellectual sloth. On the day of judgement they will perhaps weigh far more heavily than any sin of frailty. I appeal to you to establish a priority in your research.

To my great surprise, the reaction was so favourable that the congress conceived the idea of establishing an interdisciplinary and international symposium.

I went to England to discuss that particular plan with an eminent gynaecologist. Together we drew up the project of a symposium of doctors and moralists, to be held a year later. Its theme was 'Birth-Control – but How?' Such a symposium would enable doctors, psychiatrists and philosophers to put forward their particular viewpoints which, being complementary, would all contribute to the solution. And in fact, since 1959, fifty to sixty experts from a wide variety of countries have held an annual symposium at Louvain to explore the diverse aspects of human sexuality from a scientific and Christian standpoint.

And are you still the Chairman of these symposiums?

No. I served as Chairman for about fifteen years, then I came mainly to open and close the conference. I should add that this initiative led to the founding of the *Institut des Sciences Familiales et Sexologiques*, now attached to the University of Louvain.

Your basic work – and also perhaps the most important – appeared in 1955 under the title The Gospel to Every Creature. *The Preface to the Italian edition was written by the Cardinal of Milan, Giovanni Battista Montini, who later became Pope Paul VI. He called your book 'courageous', 'disturbing' and 'optimistic'. Many people have described it as the 'Suenens Manifesto'. It was ahead of its time and already anticipated the Council.*

When I wrote the book I obviously had no foreknowledge of a Second Vatican Council. But I already understood clearly that we're created not only to know and serve God, but also to help others to know him, to love and serve him. That's why my book mainly emphasized the 'how and why' of spreading the Gospel. I wanted to stress the importance of the evangelizing mission, which unfortunately is still advancing too slowly because of the inertia and indifference of countless Christians, as opposed to the real sense of commitment displayed by Communists or by the followers of this or that sect.

In 1962 you published The Nun in the World, *a book that attracted much attention and was translated into several languages.*

That book, based on a few practical experiments carried out in my diocese, aimed to free the life of nuns belonging to active orders from several outmoded customs and practices which were really hampering the apostolate. The French title, *Promotion apostolique de la religieuse*, accurately sums up the content: to brush aside the obstacles in order to serve the gospel more faithfully. Although the book was revolutionary at the time, there's nothing startling about it today. I would even say that in this work I'm more 'traditional' than many other writers, because I stress the usefulness of retaining a badge and a distinctive habit, but suitably modernized. And I think there are various good reasons for stressing the point. Pope John Paul II has expressed much the same view on several occasions. In fact, my book was urging nuns to introduce apostolic priorities in the running of their institutions: schools, hospitals, and the like.

Your latest books, such as A New Pentecost? *and* Ecumenism and Charismatic Renewal, *mainly discuss the work of the Holy Spirit in the Church.*

Certainly, because today we've reached a major turning-point in the history of the Church, and there's every indication that the Holy Spirit is renewing the face of the Church in a special way. Over the last ten years we've had a powerful institutional renewal at various levels. This renewal is now calling us to a spiritual conversion. Patriarch Athenagoras has described it very aptly: 'The situation of the modern world is one of childbirth, and childbirth always goes with hope. We contemplate the present situation with immense Christian hope and with a deep sense of responsibility for the kind of world which will emerge from today's childbearing.'

I think that the time has come for the Church to show the Christian way boldly to a pilgrim world. We all aspire to a 'new Pentecost'; for an apostolate that doesn't find its starting point in the Holy Spirit is a fruitless one. What we need is a renewal of spiritual energy. My latest books appeal for that kind of renewal.

4

A Moderator who Made the Council
Fathers Laugh

*On 19 March 1962, you received the cardinal's hat from the
hands of Pope John XXIII. And so you were called to form part
of the College of the Holy Father's closest collaborators.*

I became Cardinal just three months after I was consecrated Archbishop. That it happened so soon I owe to
Pope John's personal affection: by nominating me Cardinal, he was enabling me to see him more often during
the preparatory period immediately preceding the
Council.

And how were these more frequent contacts first established?

In accordance with the time-honoured custom, on being
nominated Cardinal I sent the Pope a letter expressing
my gratitude and obedience. With it I enclosed my first
pastoral letter to my diocese. John XXIII once confided
to me that he had read that pastoral with interest and
had felt deeply drawn to its author. Some weeks later,
when I wrote another pastoral letter on the future of the
Council, John XXIII told me that it outlined the forth-
coming event exactly as he, too, envisaged it.

All this enabled us to discuss the subject more
thoroughly and even led to his request that I work out
a plan for the Council. I had informed him that, in my
view, the seventy-two preparatory schemata were really

stodgy and without cohesion. So I tried to reduce them to a total of thirteen, without modifying their original contents for fear of offending the authors. But obviously I was attempting the impossible. I therefore drafted a new project centred on the theme of the Church *ad intra* and *ad extra*, in other words, the Church searching itself and looking outward to the world. This document, which received the approval of John XXIII, was basic to my public intervention of 4 December 1962, which all the Council Fathers subsequently approved.

May I ask you what prompted you to make that public intervention, which proved decisive and received the full support of Cardinals Montini and Lercaro on the very next day?

As you know, some rather stormy discussions had been held during the first weeks of the Council. No one could foresee their ultimate issue. It was then that John XXIII fell seriously ill. What was to happen to my project? I knew that it was still lying on the Pope's desk. Should I submit it to the Council? This would require the Holy Father's approval and support, which couldn't be obtained in view of his state of health. He'd grown so weak that I couldn't even visit him. So I decided to send him a personal letter. I still remember that day clearly: it was a Sunday. I wrote, 'We love you dearly and are praying for your speedy recovery!' Meanwhile I gave his secretary my intervention which I had outlined in writing, for I'd made up my mind to make a solemn appeal to the Council Fathers, urging them to concentrate on the theme of the Church.

The surprise came on the following day. Early in the morning I was summoned to the Vatican. Monsignor Dell'Aqua was holding the copy of my speech in his hand. I noticed that the Pope had annotated it. Though confined to his bed, he had read my draft intervention

25

and declared that he gave it his full support. I left the text with Monsignor Dell'Aqua, requesting that the Pope's annotations be translated accurately into Latin. Obviously, I was hoping that my manuscript would be returned to me eventually, but you can be sure that it will lie in the Vatican archives for another fifty years!

Well then, encouraged in my project, I submitted the draft, as approved by John XXIII, to the Assembly on 4 December 1962. There and then I received the support of Cardinals Montini and Lercaro. The course was now set and the basic theme accepted by the Council was 'the Church examining itself and its relation to the world'.

Now I won't give you a summary of the Council's proceedings: obviously, it isn't easy to sum up in a few words the work of four years, fifteen hundred public interventions, over one hundred thousand motions or written amendments, and about five hundred and twenty hours of deliberations. The major document was issued under the title *Lumen Gentium*. This text, devoted to the very mystery of the Church, dominates the other documents as Mont Blanc towers over the Alps. It's a key document which reveals to the faithful the Church's view on the prospect of a new Pentecost.

And how would you sum up this view?

You can look at the Church from outside, like a tourist visiting a cathedral. He sees its structure, its design, its columns and capitals. But you can also approach it from within, and so discover its essence: the hidden sanctuary which is the foundation of its existence. In its Constitution on the Church, the Council didn't want to stop short at the external appearance, I mean the juridical and sociological aspects. It wished to penetrate to the inmost depths of the mystery of the Church. For the faithful, this means Christ himself, who mysteriously lives in the Church and always remains just as close to it throughout the centuries.

In the *ad extra* dialogue the main question was, 'How does the Church carry out its mission in the world? What is its attitude to the human person, social justice, evangelization, world peace?'

To conclude, the project made provisions for ecumenical dialogue with all Christians. This was the subject of the conciliar decree *Unitatis Redintegratio*.

And how would you describe the bishops' relations with the Protestant and Orthodox observers at the Council?

We lived in a climate of openness, mutual regard and friendship. Our good relationships have continued to progress since the Council. Admittedly, we're still trying our wings at the doctrinal level, but we've made giant strides from the standpoint of personal contacts. On one occasion, Pope John XXIII asked the President of the World Methodist Conference, 'How much longer will our separation last?' Somewhat embarrassed, he replied, 'We've been separated for four centuries. It will probably take us another two to be reunited.' Whereupon John XXIII said with a warm smile, 'At any rate, you and I already are!' A passionate desire has materialized: the longing to behold the visible unity of all Christians. I'm convinced that no difficulty can ever again stand in the way of this ideal, however, long, however arduous at times, our postconciliar path to unity may still prove to be.

So the Council and all its results could be described as a 'surprise of the Holy Spirit'.

That's exactly what we felt it to be: a deeper discovery

of the Church and the world, an invitation to renewal in the theological, pastoral and spiritual sense. How much it enriched each one of us! Often we felt the close presence of the Holy Spirit in our midst. A theologian of the Secretariat for Unity once called the Council a Copernican revolution, because the emphasis was laid on the people of God whom the apostolic function was called to serve. The Council was a divine grace, an outstanding ecclesial and collegial event. Even if we bishops hadn't drafted a single text, the very fact that a Council was convoked showed that the Church is founded on visible collegiality. It would have been pointless to convoke 2,500 bishops to Rome had the Pope been their one and only authority. The First Vatican Council emphasized the role of the Pope; we stressed the words '*with* the Pope'. Our present task is to make both aspects blend harmoniously.

During the second Session, you were one of the four Moderators of the Council. How did this come about, and what could you do in that capacity to ensure that the working sessions would be fruitful?

At the first Session, the presidency of the Council wasn't yet running smoothly. In fact, ten Cardinals were taking turns to act as President. What we lacked was a stable presidency. Paul VI wanted to remedy this defect. At first, he thought of appointing two papal legates, but the ecclesiastical jurists objected that the idea of a legate actually in Rome was inapplicable, since the title can be attributed only to a papal delegate sent from the city of Rome on a mission. So Pope Paul said to me, 'I intend to appoint you Moderator, together with Cardinals Agagianian and Döpfner.'

Then we were joined by Cardinal Lercaro of Bologna. Döpfner, Lercaro and I were great friends. We had the same views and ideas. Agagianian, as a member of the Curia, didn't always share our outlook, but our relations were friendly.

Practically every morning, the press photographers would come to take pictures of the Moderators. The press used to judge by our expressions whether the Council was going well or badly! I would often say to Döpfner, 'Let's look cheerful, otherwise all the news reports will be gloomy.'

I think that the Pope would have liked to give us more authority over the direction and development of the Council's proceedings. But the Curia had reacted to this proposal by clamping down on it. Ultimately our function was reduced to that of presiding over the working sessions. But we always had the invaluable possibility of meeting the Pope for one or two hours a week to discuss the events as they unfolded. This constant dialogue with the Holy Father was helpful and beneficial.

Were there any events that necessitated your intervention in a more unusual way?

I remember one event very clearly because it made such a deep impression on me. Once, as we were closing a working session, the hope was expressed that the Theological Commission would declare itself on the problem of episcopal collegiality. Now, because the Theological Commission needed certain additional guidelines, I announced, as Moderator, that we would hand the bishops a questionnaire with a view to a vote that would orientate the Theological Commission and enable it to work in accordance with the expressed opinions of the Council Fathers. But instead of taking that questionnaire to the printer, the messenger took it to the Holy Office! For two whole weeks we Moderators were on tenterhooks. At long last, a commission of twenty-eight Cardinals met to decide whether or not we had the right to ask those questions, which were decisive for the future of the debate on collegiality.

We finally won the battle. Two unforeseeable incidents acted in our favour; the Holy Spirit is a great one for surprises! In the first place, Cardinal Tisserant came to our aid unknowingly by getting the wrong end of the question. Instead of asking, 'Are the Moderators entitled to hand round these questionnaires?', he instantly exclaimed, 'I think that the whole thing is couched incorrectly', and instead of looking at the questions, began to correct the Latin in which we had formulated them.

Next, we gained a favourable vote because another Cardinal, who was a bit hard of hearing, misunderstood the issue. So he voted for the questionnaire and, by that very fact, in favour of collegiality.

May I ask who that Cardinal was?

Well, I've always said that I wouldn't reveal his name during his lifetime, but now that he's gone to heaven, I can tell you that it was Cardinal Spellman. So he unwittingly became the instrument of an original manifestation of the Holy Spirit on that occasion.

Among your interventions, three have become famous. They concern the restoration of the permanent diaconate, the charisms of the whole people of God, and the retirement of church dignitaries at the age of seventy-five. What prompted you to make those interventions?

I had long been convinced of the necessity of restoring the permanent diaconate, as it has always existed in the Eastern Churches. I had in mind regions like Latin America, but also other parts of the world. The diaconate is all part of the sacramental armour of the Church. It was sad to think that such a grace for the ministry of souls was being neglected. I felt that the dogmatic aspect of the question was important. Some may ask, why do we need deacons in the Church? To understand the significance of the diaconate, you have to view it under the sacramental aspect which makes it a distinctive function. At first, my proposal met with strong opposition and, curiously enough, from the bishops of Africa as well. There were even some Latin American bishops who feared that it would cause a decline in the priestly vocation. And there was yet another anxiety: might not the married deacon be the first step towards the married priest? Admittedly, all these fears were to some extent legitimate. But, I asked, should we, in the Church, let ourselves be guided by fear?

And how do you explain that, despite all these hesitations, the Council decided to restore the permanent diaconate?

I can only say that, in the heat of the debate, I was careful to add: 'No one is obliged to introduce the permanent diaconate in his diocese. All I request is that those who consider it useful should be free to introduce it.' I think that my remark helped us to reach agreement over this issue.

How do you envisage the deacon's task in today's world?

Obviously, it's difficult to justify the necessity of the deacon if one considers only his liturgical function; for to envisage him as a mere assistant to the parish priest in the administration of the sacraments is a far too narrow view. The deacon's vocation is to serve as a link between the Church and those who are on the fringe of it, or have become estranged from it. In my own diocese

31

we have seventy deacons for seventeen hundred priests. This proportion is, I believe, one of the highest in the Church. I've personally ordained those deacons in their villages or home towns and I'm proud of them. In this way I've been able to nominate deacons for specialized ministries, such as the care of prisoners, invalids, the young, and so on. For example, we have two deacons serving at Brussels Airport. Without a doubt, we need even more imagination, even more creativity, in the way we implement this new ministry in the Church.

On 22 October 1963, during the debate on the Schema De Ecclesia *you pointed out that too little importance was being accorded to the charism of the faithful in that document.*

At first I had no intention of intervening on this subject. But when I heard a Cardinal say that, in his view, the gifts of the Holy Spirit had been destined only for the primitive Church, I felt obliged to intervene. For such a denial of the actuality of the charisms was making the real spiritual awakening of the whole people of God virtually impossible. In doing so, the Church would be overlooking the deep significance of the fact that the Holy Spirit works actively in each human being. I asked a theologian to collect for me and analyse all the important texts on the charisms. Then I made my intervention:

> It is dangerous to believe that the hierarchy is no more than an administrative apparatus. Without the gifts of the Holy Spirit, the ecclesiastical function would be impoverished and fruitless. The two thousand years that have elapsed since our Lord's ascension have always been 'times of the Holy Spirit'. The charisms are not just the extraordinary gifts, like prophecy, healing and so on. Paul also speaks of the

more general gifts, such as the ministerial charism, the gift of service. The Holy Spirit bestows his grace on each one of us, although he expresses himself in a variety of ways. All Christians have to co-operate with him in a living, active and responsible manner. But because the individual is a member of Christ's body, he must exercise his gifts in a way that harmonizes with the gifts of others. Realities like the people of God, the body of Christ, will remain purely theological abstractions unless they're vivified by the power of the Holy Spirit. Priests, bishops and the Pope, in fellowship with the laity, form the people of God. And if this people is to be seen as an active reality, we need the Holy Spirit's action in the life of the Church. It wasn't only in past centuries, in the time of St Thomas Aquinas or St Francis of Assisi for example, that the gifts of God's grace were needed. We still need them today.

During the Council you often emerged as a controversial figure. What did you feel then about that role?

Obviously, it wasn't an easy role, nor had I sought to play it. But when I saw that a proposal, an idea, served the common good and the Church, I felt it my duty to say so, despite all the difficulties that plain speaking might entail. My public interventions also stemmed from my permanent conviction that the Church is a family, and that in a family you can express yourself frankly and freely.

It was you, too, who made the Council Fathers laugh for the first time in history.

Yes, this was during my intervention on the desirability of dispensing wich such solemn addresses as

'Eminentissimi' and 'Reverendissimi'. I said to the Council Fathers:

> Dear brothers in Christ, unless I am mistaken, nowhere is it written in holy Scripture that the apostles used the title 'Eminence' among themselves. And I can hardly imagine that Peter and Paul asked others to call them 'Eminentissimi'. Besides, if we dispense with such titles, we can save valuable time for discussion.

Well, for the first time in history, this raised a burst of laughter in the Council. I'm still proud of that achievement, because it isn't easy to make a Council laugh.

And such spontaneity is certainly very important for brotherly dialogue.

Of course it is. I cherish a very happy memory of 'Bar Jonas', where the bishops would meet quite informally and chat over their capuccinos.

On 11 November 1963 you proposed that an age-limit of seventy-five be set for the retirement of bishops.

Yes. I realized that in doing this I could lose favour among my colleagues. But I believed that when something is in the best interests of the Church, it has to be stated, regardless of the reactions! I prayed earnestly to the Holy Spirit; then I felt a great inner assurance and I made up my mind to speak. I said:

> There is every indication that the Council is giving the bishop greater responsibility. So he will need greater physical fitness. For it is primarily on him that the animation and development of apostolic work, and the transformation of the Church into a mission field,

will depend. The sociological evolution of our time needs to be kept up at a dynamic rhythm. One has to be young – in body and mind – to cope with ever-new situations.

Then an objection was raised: 'A bishop is indissolubly united to his diocese by a mystical bond.' To this I replied, 'We had better not resort to the argument of the mystical marriage; for among this illustrious Assembly I can see many bishops who have changed their sees more than once and are therefore divorced.' My initial proposal had been to make seventy the age of retirement, but realizing that the opposition was fierce, I extended it to seventy-five. In spite of this, the Assembly was prepared to accept only a vaguely worded text, with no clearly specified age-limit. I protested vigorously, 'If the age-limit is not specified here and now, that wording is no more than a drop in the ocean.' This was greeted with stony silence.

How did Cardinal Montini react to your proposal?

On the day of his election, Paul VI said to me, 'What a pity we didn't fix the age-limit there and then. . . .' Six months later, he settled the question himself in his *Motu Proprio*. When I reached the age of seventy-five on 16 July 1979, I too had to comply with this decision. And I'm glad of it, because the Church must remain young and be constantly regenerated by new blood.

5

A Friend
of Several Popes

Pope John XXIII's affection for you doubtless explains why he sent you to the United Nations as his ambassador on 13 May 1963. On that occasion you presented to the UN Assembly his encyclical Pacem in Terris, *which has been called his last will and testament.*

That confidential mission is one of my most treasured memories, not only because of its importance, but also because of the great trust Pope John had placed in me.

And in addressing the UN Assembly, what had you really set your heart on achieving?

My chief aim was to present clearly the unique nature of the encyclical. For Pope John hadn't addressed it to Catholics alone. He'd written it as an open letter to all men of good will. In this he was witnessing to his love for all mankind. The basic theme of the encyclical, I explained to the Assembly, is like a symphony of peace. And peace is built on truth, its foundation; on justice, its main rule; on love, its motive force; on freedom, its living space. Peace demands respect for individuals. Here I quoted Antoine de Saint-Exupéry: 'When respect for man will come to dwell in our hearts, then and only then will we be able to devise a social, political and economic system that embraces respect for each living being.' I pointed out to the Assembly that peace begins in our hearts, but that it must ripple outward in ever-widening concentric circles to the limits of the universe. And I added:

> No person of good will can be resigned to the fact that two men out of three are starving. Civilization is unworthy of its name if it remains indifferent to this collective social sin. We are still far removed from mutual understanding and a true spirit of friendship. We pass one another by, without so much as a greeting, a smile. The men of our century have discovered interplanetary space, but they have scarcely begun to explore the space which separates them from each other. They have built gigantic bridges across rivers, but they have not yet learned to bridge the gap that separates nation from nation. True, our century has discovered nuclear energy, but it has not yet discovered the creative energy that resides in peace and concord.

The whole encyclical aims to make the world a better place to live in.

After your address, you faced a barrage of questions. You were asked, I believe, whether women also have a role to play in the endeavour to establish world peace?

Yes. I replied by quoting Lenin: 'Revolution without women is inconceivable.' And I added, 'If women are necessary for a revolution to succeed, they are equally necessary for the establishment of peace.' That's why I then gave a direct message to all women: 'Women of the world, we need you!'

The interviewers were also very interested in the Pope's attitude to the world. One of them asked, 'Is it

true that John XXIII gives his blessing to Communism?'
I replied:

> Communism includes three elements: the principles, the movement and men. As for the principles, the Pope cannot give his blessing to them, for they are incompatible with the Church's doctrine. As for the movement, Communism is more or less imbued with its own ideological teaching. But as for men, certainly the Pope loves them, for they are often much better than their principles. . . .

At the beginning of the second Session of the Council, John XXIII died. On 28 October 1963, Paul VI asked you to deliver the commemorative oration in honour of this man to whom you were so deeply attached.

For me, this was a unique opportunity to pay homage to him. I sent Paul VI a wire, asking 'What language? How long?' He wired back, 'Language up to you. Time 45 minutes.' Since I decided to speak in French, Latin was dispensed with for the first time as the official language of the conciliar assembly.

And how did you pay homage to John XXIII in that historic address?

I tried to express what Pope John had been to me: a father, perhaps also a grandfather; a wise old man in whose presence one could feel relaxed and at peace. He himself was so unselfconscious as a Pope that he once said to me jokingly, 'I still can't understand why I was made Pope: I imagine that even God can't work it out.' With the same sense of fun, he once said that an angel had appeared to him in a dream and told him not to worry too much about his responsibilities. 'After all,' said the angel, 'you're only the Pope!' And while telling this story, he was shaking with laughter.

When the Council resumed its deliberations, we had to get used to the idea, very gradually, that we would never again see in our midst that kindly face, that bright smile, those warm, welcoming gestures. John XXIII was at once amazingly natural and supernatural. In him nature and grace were blended into a living unity, full of incomparable spontaneity and charm. He lived in the presence of God with simplicity. He devoted himself to the everyday concerns of men with warm sympathy. He knew how to listen to a child, how to comfort an invalid. He would be interested in the building of an airport, and he would pray for the astronauts. But, at the same time, he lived in the intimacy of the angels and the saints. He surprised even St Joseph by including him in the canon of the Mass. In him there was no duality, nature and grace were perfectly united. He brought light to mankind through his very life, as the sun brightens and warms the earth. His spontaneous, direct goodness dispelled the mists, melted the ice, almost imperceptibly. He was like a sunbeam, radiating optimism and bringing joy by his mere presence.

John XXIII was not so naive as to believe that goodness can solve all problems. But he knew that it opens hearts to dialogue, to understanding and mutual esteem. He knew that truth penetrates deeper into the minds of men when it comes to them as a revelation of love.

Pope John helped us to understand the meaning of loving one's neighbour no matter what the cost, that is, to devote one's complete attention to the existence of another person. Because of this basic wisdom, he always spoke of himself with a dash of humour. His life has been a grace for the world. He was a pope of dialogue. His words left a permanent echo. In him men recognized a voice speaking to them of God, but also of human brotherhood, of the need to restore social justice and peace to the whole world. They heard a voice that appealed to the best in them; they lifted up their eyes to this man whose goodness gave them a foreknowledge of God.

He loved children; he befriended the poor, who would look out for the kind face of this old man, knowing that he was one of them. He was the friend of the prisoners whom he had visited in *Regina Coeli*, the Roman prison, and had encouraged by his presence. Among them were two convicted murderers. One of them approached Pope John and asked, 'Are your words of hope also meant for a great sinner like me?' John XXIII replied simply by opening his arms and embracing him.

The last weeks of the Pope's life were darkened by his serious illness.

A few months before his death he said, 'I know what my personal contribution to the successful conclusion of the Council will be. It will be suffering.' And it wasn't difficult to guess what he meant by that: his imminent death. He believed from the depths of his soul in the spiritual value of the supreme sacrifice wholeheartedly accepted. During one of his last audiences, he said, 'All days are good for being born, all days are good for dying. I know in whom I have believed. This is what matters.' He welcomed his earthly death with the serene joy of a child returning to his father's house. For all of us, his death was like the celebration of an Easter liturgy.

When did you see him for the last time?

Towards the end of January 1963. It was an unexpected, informal meeting. I encountered Don Capovilla, the Pope's private secretary, in the Basilica of St Peter. He asked me to come up with him to his office. There he handed me a present from the Pope. It was a signed photograph of John XXIII with me kneeling before him. I had forgotten on that occasion that Cardinals don't kneel before the Pope. At the back of the photo Pope John had written *Non placet mihi* – 'I do not approve!' It was one of the last expressions of his great sense of humour. Then the secretary took me into the Holy Father's private room. We spoke together for two hours, and I treasure that conversation as one of the most unforgettable encounters of my life.

In your relationship with Paul VI, you've often been compared to the apostle Paul, who wasn't afraid to disagree openly with Peter.

During the four years of the Council, I was often asked to communicate to him the bishops' real opinions on this or that subject. Obviously, this wasn't easy. I would often think of the words of Patriarch Athenagoras: 'The Pope needs brothers who have the courage to speak to him in all sincerity.' Clearly, this calls for great mutual trust. At times there were painful differences of opinion between Paul VI and myself, but these in no way affected my loyalty to the Pope or my faith in him.

Since the Church is also a human institution, it is, of course, in a state of perpetual transformation. That's perfectly natural. It lives in history and in time. It's influenced by the society that surrounds it. You have only to enter a cathedral to see what I mean by the mark of centuries. Under the romanesque or gothic arches, you find the adornments of various ages: renaissance decorations, rococo or stucco ornamentations. These decorations aren't an integral part of the cathedral. They cover and conceal the original walls. In the same way, the Church must constantly cast off the accretions and trammels of its own history. It must rediscover its original identity: a presence of God, far removed from every form of triumphalism, superficiality and extraneous power.

One can criticise the performance of a car without criticizing the driver. I once presented my secretary, Canon Brieven, to Pope Paul, with the words, 'Holy Father, this is my secretary. Not only does he attend to all my correspondence, but he also drives me around the chaotic streets of Rome – and that isn't easy!' Smiling, the Pope replied, 'Being the driver of the Church of God isn't easy either.'

Paul VI was very keenly aware of his responsibility. He often seemed to be weighed down by this awareness. He used to write his own speeches with great care. I once said to him, 'Holy Father, why don't you improvise a little?' But it was really difficult for him to do this, for he believed that the Pope's words should be so carefully weighed and pondered that they would be beyond criticism. Representing the papacy, he always kept foremost in his mind his fidelity to his vocation: 'Do you love me more than these others do?' As the successor of Peter, he loved his Master passionately and served him to the point of exhaustion. He was unswervingly devoted to God and mankind. And he retained this unswerving devotion, in particularly harrowing circumstances and in a world torn by ever-increasing suffering, want, insecurity, hatred, terrorism and violations of human rights.

He seized every opportunity to raise his voice and proclaim the gospel message: peace, concern for others, goodness, mutual understanding, predilection for the poor. Addressing the United Nations, he begged the Assembly to do away permanently with fratricidal warfare. He adjured the implacable terrorists to end the sufferings of his friend Aldo Moro. He offered his own life in exchange for the release of the hostages of Mogadishu. He raised his voice whenever the situation demanded it, regardless of his own safety.

He also ran the risk of being strongly criticized. I can testify how generously and conscientiously he fulfilled his duty to humanity. He loved the human race with a deep and sensitive compassion. 'What can I do to help you?' was a question that cropped up frequently in his conversations with others. His love for mankind impelled him to travel all over the world: from America to Africa, from the Near East to India. As long as he could make his presence felt as a force for peace, he never spared himself.

When in January 1964 Paul VI landed at Amman Airport, in the course of his pilgrimage to the holy places, 90% of the crowd waiting there to greet him were Muslims and Jews. He was the first Pope since Peter to have walked along the streets of Jerusalem towards the Mount of Olives. Later, when he participated in the World Eucharistic Congress at Bombay, he was again greeted by an enthusiastic crowd, and this time 90% of the throng were Hindus. The reason why Pope Paul touched the hearts of non-Christians was that his concern was not limited to his own flock but extended to all men. Never shall I forget that face, drawn and haggard by suffering, which revealed, more eloquently than any words could, the price he had to pay for loving and serving mankind.

Paul VI not only bore the burden of human distress, but also knew how to lead the Church when it was undergoing painful upheavals. He had the unenviable task of implementing the work of Vatican II at a time when serious religious crises were undermining the very roots of our faith. Tirelessley, he would serve each Wednesday as the spokesman of his Master and remind the world of the essential truths of the Christian life.

History will have to acknowledge how loyally he pursued the work of spiritual and structural renewal, already begun by Vatican II. He looked for a happy medium between progressives and conservatives, striving to find a common denominator. His faith was the secret of his perseverance and apostolic courage from the beginning to the end of his pontificate.

Shortly before his death, I sent him the complete American edition of his own speeches and writings on the Holy Spirit. This work alone shows, by its volume as much as by its content, how deeply and permanently the Holy Spirit inspired his life.

It was equally Paul VI, I believe, who asked you to help him blend the charismatic Church and the institutional Church into one family.

Yes. I shall never forget our encounter on the occasion of the Conference on Charismatic Renewal during Holy Year, that is, in 1975. I presented about ten thousand participants to the Pope. Paul VI looked at me for a while, then he said, 'I thank you in the name of Christ for your efforts on behalf of the Charismatic Movement, and I would like you to devote yourself to its complete integration into the Church.'

And your last contact with him?

It was in the form of a personal letter dated 27 May 1978. In his letter he thanked me once again for my efforts to incorporate the Charismatic Movement into the life of the Church. 'We are happy', he wrote, 'to tell you today how much we appreciate these efforts. We pray the Lord to fill you with his grace in your service to the Church.' For me, those lines have the force of a farewell and a testament. This was the last exchange in

a relationship of friendship and trust which we had
enjoyed for over thirty years.

*And how would you describe your relationship with Pope John
Paul I?*

Before his election we used to meet only on the occasion
of the Roman Synods, and we would always greet one
another warmly. I once offered to send him my book *A
New Pentecost?*, '. . . but', I said, 'only on condition that
you write and tell me what you think about it.' Accord-
ingly, he sent me a very kind letter, which was already
indicative of the endearing nature of the 'smiling Pope'.

And may I ask you what he said in his letter?

He wrote:

> Dear Cardinal, you have the gift of writing convinc-
> ingly and in a way that stimulates my curiosity. As to
> form and content, your book has prompted me to
> reread St Paul's texts with new eyes, although I
> thought that I was already well acquainted with them.
> Through your book, the Acts of the Apostles have
> become an even more valuable guide for me. I thank
> you for the good you have done my soul. I also thank
> you for your stimulating service to the Church.

Immediately after his election, I approached him
spontaneously to thank him, in my turn, for his courageous acceptance of the ministry of Peter. His answer to
the assembled Cardinals was, 'May God forgive you for
what you have done to me!' But he said it with that
well-known smile.

The Mass which Pope John Paul II celebrated on acceding to the

45

ministry of Peter was followed on television by millions of people. During this first contact with the world – literally 'the world', since over eighty television chains retransmitted the event around the globe – the Holy Father said these memorable words: 'Fear not to welcome Christ and accept his power!' How would you interpret this exhortation?

We who desire to serve Christ, with the Pope, must all open our doors to him: the frontiers of states, scientific and political systems, the spheres of culture, civilization and development. Man is so often unaware of what lies in the inmost depths of his mind and heart. He begins to have doubts about the meaning of life, he falls prey to uncertainty. John Paul II is taking us by the hand, as it were, and directing our gaze to the one who is the fulfilment of our faith and of whom he's the spokesman and the humble servant: Jesus Christ.

Pope John Paul II repeated this heartfelt cry in his encyclical Redemptor Hominis.

Yes, the Pope loves to encounter 'the man of today'. He goes out to greet him with love and hope. In his encyclical he's addressing all men, for he says, 'Christ is united with each man, without any exception whatever, even when man is unaware of it.' In this the Pope sees the deepest foundation of mutual respect, for each man is a unique being of inestimable value.

So the encyclical Redemptor Hominis *is appealing to all of us to renew and strengthen our faith?*

Exactly. The encyclical is also urging us to become more conscious of what being a Christian means. Now that I'm about to retire as a bishop, I want to repeat to the young the Holy Father's message at the beginning of his pontificate: 'Never be afraid to welcome Christ and his power!'

If we consider the full implications of this message, we have to admit that there's only one perfect Christian: Christ himself. But we can allow ourselves to be transformed by him so that we may receive something of his fullness. To live in Jesus Christ means to see with his eyes, to speak with his lips and to walk in his footsteps.

6

A Charismatic
Prompted by the Holy Spirit

Cardinal, fifteen years have elapsed since the closing of Vatican Council II. What would you say of the Council in retrospect?

I'd like to resort to an analogy to explain how I view the results achieved so far. If you're waiting for a lift on the ground floor of a building and the indicator tells you it's stopped on the sixth floor, you may say, 'It's already come down to the sixth floor.' But if you're waiting for that same lift on the twenty-fifth floor, you'll probably say, 'It's still way down on the sixth floor.' So the answer to your question depends on one's standpoint. The Council was a great moment in the history of the Church. Thanks to the Council, our vision of the Church has gained in balance, and also in breadth. But the transposition of the Council's achievements into our everyday life is by no means completed. With the Council, the Church began to move forward, and nothing can ever again halt that momentum. As Patriarch Athenagoras once said, 'The Holy Spirit has opened doors that no one can ever close again.'

The Council is continued in a special way through the Synod of Bishops, which meets at regular intervals in Rome. How do you envisage the function of the Synod?

As an instrument for participation in the leadership of

the whole Church, the Synod of Bishops can certainly be developed further. Besides, when he was still Patriarch of Venice, Pope John Paul I had urged the 1971 Synod to improve the assembly's procedural method. Soon after his election, the *Osservatore Romano* reprinted that speech, which suggests that he was determined to change the procedure of the Synod. John Paul II will very probably do so, because there's room for much improvement.

What have you in mind, for example?

I would say that the Synod's standing council, which consists of twelve elected members and three appointed by the Pope, is capable of working more effectively in the future. That council has to maintain a continuity between the Synods, which are held every three years. We'd have better results, I feel, if the standing council could meet more often – say three times a year for a whole week – in order to deliberate with the Pope on the guidelines to be adopted. At the same time, this would ensure both the successful preparation and the efficient running of the following Synod.

We also have to find a more efficient working method. For example, each representative of an Episcopal Conference is allowed eight minutes in which to address the Assembly. This procedure is repeated one hundred and twenty times. The working sessions would already be less cumbersome if each representative submitted his intervention in writing, perhaps even a month in advance. The full or abridged texts could then be published. In this way, the participants could familiarize themselves with the contents and approach the problems with full knowledge of the facts.

I often find that we bishops, too, need to relearn each day to be more open to the Holy Spirit and less concerned with defending our viewpoints. It certainly isn't easy, but it's only by really listening to God's voice that we're able to understand his plans for the renewal of the Church.

Another problem, in my view, lies in the way the Synod works in groups. These are, in effect, language groups. I feel that this isn't the most effective method. The discussion groups should be determined by the very nature of the problems examined. For instance, in our French-speaking group we had Cardinal Marty of France, two bishops from Vietnam and four Africans. Certainly we were speaking the same language, but our pastoral problems were as varied as the colour of our skins.

Wasn't Cardinal Wojtyla in your group on several occasions?

Yes, he participated in it on the occasion of the first four Synods, but not during the last one. I asked him, 'Cardinal, why have you left our French group?' – 'Well,' he replied, 'I've decided to join the Italian group.' – 'Why so?' – 'Because the Italians have a problem with Communists. Perhaps I can be of help to them through our own experience in Poland.'

Do you think that one day we'll have an Ecumenical Council in the full sense of the word, that is, a Council in which the other Churches would no longer be passive observers but active participants, headed by the Pope, the Patriarch of Constantinople, the Archbishop of Canterbury, and so on?

Perhaps such a Council presupposes an even greater openness to the breath of the Spirit. But, above all, our dialogue for unity can't be a dialogue between Rome and Canterbury, Rome and Moscow, Rome and Constantinople. It must be a dialogue between Rome and

Christ, Canterbury and Christ, Moscow and Christ. Perhaps that great day will dawn for us by the end of the century. Certain signs seem to be pointing in this direction, such as the preparation of a Panorthodox Council of the Eastern Churches. I think that Jerusalem would be the ideal place for such an event: the city of the first Council of the Apostles, the cradle of the Church, the city where the first Eucharist was celebrated and where the apostles, with Mary the mother of Jesus, received the Holy Spirit. As T. S. Eliot says so beautifully in *Four Quartets*:

> We shall not cease from exploration
> And the end of all our exploring
> Will be to arrive where we started
> And know the place for the first time.

Of course, it's a dream, but we have to dream. The words of a Brazilian song come to my mind: 'When a man dreams alone, it is only a dream. But when several dream the same dream, then a new world begins.'

When you celebrated your priestly jubilee in 1977, you went on a pilgrimage to Jerusalem. Was that a prophetic gesture?

Above all, I wanted to give due thanks to the Lord for the many manifestations of his grace over those fifty years. What place could have been more appropriate than the Cenacle in Jerusalem, and what time more suitable than Pentecost? So I set out for the Holy Land with a group of fifty-two pilgrims, all friends of mine. Three-quarters of them were not Catholics: they had joined me because they all shared my wish to celebrate in Jerusalem a kind of anticipation of a new Pentecost for the Church.

Your concern for Christian Unity has been one of the driving forces of your life. As we all know, you formed close ties with many representatives of other confessions during Vatican II. Did these relationships bear fruit?

On the last day of the Council, a group of Protestants from the United States spontaneously approached me and invited me to a farewell dinner. I readily accepted their invitation. During the dinner they said to me:

> We've completely changed our ideas about the Catholic Church. We've lived with you as brothers for four years. But our brothers in America haven't had the joy of such an experience. Of course, they know that a Council has been held, but that's about all they know. Couldn't you visit us in the States and tell the students in our universities about the new image of the Catholic Church and its presence in the world, so that you could discuss all these things with them?

I could hardly have refused such a kind invitation, so I accepted it. At first I thought it would entail just one visit. But over the last fifteen years I've visited the States again and again. This has led to a vast network of friendly relationships and innumerable encounters.

And also, I imagine, to deep friendships with the representatives of a wide variety of confessions.

But of course! For example, I've formed a deep friendship with Dr Outler, one of the most eminent theologians of the Methodist Church. And, obviously, with many others. Besides, a vast network of warm ecumenical relationships has grown within the Charismatic Movement: with Lutherans, Pentecostals, Presbyterians, and so on. All these relationships have kept me very occupied since the Council.

And even when our dialogue wasn't confined to strictly theological matters, we were all struck – perhaps for that very reason – by the great openness and the remarkable ease with which we discussed things together. I remember, for instance, a dinner at Chicago University where the guests, including some of the Professors, were sitting at several tables. I was telling my table a few anecdotes about Pope John and everyone was laughing heartily. The other guests noticed our mirth, and one of them asked me, 'Won't you let us all in on these stories?' So I interrupted my meal and spoke to them at length about John XXIII. You see, simply by talking about his life, a new image of the papacy was taking shape.

These journeys and conferences really are a unique opportunity to present the new image of the Catholic Church to the members of other confessions.

Of course. And to do so in an atmosphere of friendship. No one doubts my catholicity, so I can discuss delicate subjects without any difficulty.

A new ecumenical event is the common celebration of Pentecost. In 1978 a congress of this type was held in the United States and seventy thousand people participated in it. It was also attended by Cardinal Cooke and several other bishops. In 1979 there was an important ecumenical celebration of Pentecost in twenty-seven American cities, and also in England, Ireland and other countries. Even if we haven't yet achieved eucharistic intercommunion, we can already be united at this level. I have personally participated in such a congress in the State of Oklahoma. I have great confidence in this new breath of the Holy Spirit and I hope that this ecumenical celebration of Pentecost will spread from village to village, from city to city, and throughout the Church.

Together with Dr Coggan, until recently Archbishop of Canter-

*bury, you unveiled in York Minster a plaque commemorating the
Malines Conversations. Are your contacts with the Anglican
Church a direct continuation of Cardinal Mercier's work?*

Yes, indeed. This dialogue which my predecessor initiated has been pursued to this very day, but in a different
and non-official way. I'm thinking, for instance, of a
series of lectures I gave with Dr Ramsey, then Archbishop of Canterbury. We spoke to an assembly of eigh-
ty-five bishops and, subsequently, to the entire
Episcopalian clergy of New York on the theme of 'the
future of the Christian Church'. Together, Dr Ramsey
and I published our lectures under the titles *The Future
of the Christian Church* (1971) and *Come Holy Spirit* (1977).

*It's said of your diocese that it receives bishops of other confessions
more frequently than any other diocese.*

I don't really know, but it's possible. In 1967 I was the
first Catholic Cardinal since the sixteenth century to
visit the Archbishop of Canterbury and to stay at Lam-
beth Palace as his guest.

*In 1978 you were invited to preside over the great mission to the
students of Oxford University, which is held every ten years.
Usually this task falls to the Archbishop of Canterbury. It was
the first time in the history of the Anglican Church that such an
invitation was extended to a Catholic bishop.*

Yes, and of course I accepted the invitation. The students themselves proposed the theme to me: 'What Is
Your God?' For a whole week we held a religious conference each evening in Oxford's Caledonian Theatre.
Two thousand students participated in this mission. The
aim was to present the Christian faith to the members
of the University, not simply as a theory to be meditated,

but as a life-style which a person can adopt with his whole heart and mind. I tried to show that, if we want to learn to know God, we must love him and empty ourselves so that he can penetrate us; for, as St Paul says, we are called to become new creatures.

Every evening the theatre was packed, and I thank the Lord for it. For me, those mission days were days of grace.

On 19 May 1969 you gave the periodical Informations Catholiques Internationales *an interview which prompted both positive and negative reactions. Would you say that the wishes, thoughts and proposals, which you then expressed concerning the Church, have been implemented?*

With the benefit of hindsight, I would say that the most important points I made then are still of topical interest. I wanted to demonstrate Vatican II's inherent logic, as understood by the majority of the Council Fathers. The strongest reactions came from certain members of the Curia. Yet I had quoted an unequivocal statement of the Pope: 'The Curia must be grateful when a criticism is made through love of the Church.' I knew that my words would be misinterpreted. But precisely because I love the Church and the Pope, I was ready to pay the price. There are times when loyalty obliges one to speak very plainly; such criticism is another form of coresponsibility and love for the whole Church.

In that interview, you described the Pope's charism as service to the unity and fellowship of all the Churches.

When we stress the importance of episcopal collegiality, we must, at the same time, emphasize the indispensable role of the Pope as the living bond of fellowship and also as a voice capable of addressing the whole world. Today humanity is ready to listen to a man who shares and expresses its aspirations but also clearly denounces its sins: war, murder, terrorism. . . . Men are looking for someone whom they can value as a brother, a father.

This love for mankind is something we discover tangibly in John Paul II. That's why, wherever he goes, the crowds are drawn to him. Even the representatives of other confessions call him a universal pastor. As for those of us who work with the Pope, we're happy to know how much he desires to keep up the momentum of the Council. No sooner was he elected than John Paul II said to us, 'Now we are going to build up collegiality together, an effective and affective collegiality, both in our achievements and in our hearts.'

In the interview we were discussing, you also said that the internal tensions of the Church must be overcome if it desires to be a sign of unity for the world.

As long as we remain on the level of human polarizations, we won't achieve internal harmony. We have to 'put on Christ', as St Paul says, and open ourselves to his Spirit, together. As long as we remain too man-centred in our thoughts and actions, we're constantly exposed to the danger of division. I think that we have to realize, even more than we do at present, that Christian unity is a fruit of the Holy Spirit and that it isn't a work of human hands.

You once said that you have always endeavoured to obey the promptings of the Holy Spirit. This, I imagine, accounts for your close contacts with the renewal movements in the Church, such as the Focolare Movement and the Charismatic Renewal.

When, in 1972, I first made the acquaintance of Chiara Lubich, the foundress of the Focolare Movement, I was surprised to discover that the official name of her movement is 'Work of Mary', a work whose charism is unity. When names were being put forward for the 1977 Templeton Award for religious achievements, I spontaneously thought of Chiara and her work.

It's very rightly said that the future of the Church depends on the vitality of the Christian community; for Christians must demonstrate the logic of their belief by living their faith. No man can be a Christian for his sole benefit. A Christian is sustained by others and lives with others. The Focolare Movement is the embodiment of such a living community. The Focolari or 'hearths', so called because they radiate God's light and warmth, have spread throughout the world and form, as it were, microcosms of Christianity. You can't speak for three minutes with a Focolarino without the world 'love' springing quite naturally to his lips. You see, it really is his vocation to show the modern world how deeply the power of love transforms everything. And because the Focolarini take the Gospel seriously, as the word of life for today, without watering down any of it, these men and women are living witnesses to the Lord's promise, 'My words are spirit and they are life' (John 6:63). Chiara Lubich says in her writings that if all the bibles in the world were destroyed through some catastrophe, it should be possible to reconstitute the Gospel just by looking at the life of Christians.

The word of God, 'Where two or three meet in my name, I shall be there with them' (Matt. 18:20), is not only the key to their spirituality, but also the distinctive feature of their ecumenical work. On the famous occasion when Patriarch Athenagoras and Paul VI met, Chiara Lubich played an important role as an intermediary.

Besides, I believe that Chiara Lubich's movement marks an important stage in the pastoral work of today's

Church. At the Synod of Bishops in Rome, we've discussed the subject of catechesis more than once. And every time, we've all agreed that faith can best be illustrated by the catechism that Christians live. That's precisely what the Focolare communities are endeavouring to do. A few years ago, I came to know their model village in Loppiano, near Florence. The way these young people love one another is really impressive. If only more people could discover that love! Here's a small example to illustrate what I mean. Three or four years ago, I was flying from Brussels to Rome and I happened to be sitting next to a young Italian engineer. I asked him if he was a Catholic. 'I used to be,' he replied, 'but I've left the Church.' – 'Why?' – 'Because I didn't meet true Christians there.' – 'Where do you live?' – 'Near Florence.' 'In that case,' I said, 'I'll give you the address of the Loppiano model village, which is quite near your city. Go and see for yourself.'

I felt certain that the life-style of that community could be the most convincing demonstration of God's existence for that young man. I hope that the Focolare Movement will be increasingly penetrated by the Holy Spirit's power to renew the Church and the world.

Today you're closely associated with the Charismatic Movement. Why are you so deeply attached to it?

Perhaps through fidelity to the motto I chose in 1945: *in spiritu sancto.* I believe that the Charismatic Renewal is a grace which is now penetrating the whole Christian Church. It's awakening our faith in the active presence of the Holy Spirit. It's reminding Christians that the Holy Spirit is the vital breath of the Church, that the more we believe in his powerful, active presence and await it and allow it to work in us, the more it becomes effective. In every age, the Spirit speaks to his own by inspiring them in a variety of ways and in new accents, but the aim of all these promptings is that we should live the Gospel 'in spirit and in truth'. Because we're much too preoccupied with everyday happenings, it's often difficult for us to recognize the inspirations of the Holy Spirit. For he speaks gently and we have to listen attentively. We aren't naturally tuned in to his wavelength.

People often think that the Charismatic Movement essentially consists of prayer groups centred on the extraordinary charisms of which St Paul speaks. No, it's primarily an awareness of the active presence of the Holy Spirit – with all his gifts – in the heart of the Church's sacramental life and in each one of us. It's grounded in an experience of conversion to Jesus Christ, an experience that transforms the Christian life.

And surely the Charismatic Renewal is also making an enormous contribution to Christian Unity?

I believe that it's called to fulfil a special ecumenical mission, and that ecumenism will find in it the grace of deeper spiritual understanding, as a complementary gift. Naturally, the manifold work of the Holy Spirit doesn't immediately reveal itself to us in its full clarity. When you look back on events after some time has elapsed, you observe that the ecumenical current and the charismatic current basically strengthen each other, and that what you're really contemplating is one and the same work, one and the same prompting of God's Spirit, one and the same internal logic. The Church's desire to fulfil its mission, to unite all Christians and to renew its own life is one, indivisible state of being. Spreading the gospel, ecumenical vocation, renewal in the Holy Spirit – all these are intimately united. It's one and the same grace, but seen from different angles, that's all.

Cardinal, may I ask you a very personal question? Pain is something that every man experiences and which may affect him in the inmost depths of his being. What significance has the reality of suffering assumed in your own life?

If you consider pain as the seed of a new life, as the beginning of a deeper relationship with God, then I've always welcomed it as a sign of his love. Yes, even if the problem of suffering remains. Suffering is bound up with the mystery of God's love and of human freedom. Here's a thought of the poet Paul Claudel which has often brought me strength and enlightenment: 'Jesus did not come to explain and abolish suffering, but to take it up into himself and fill it with his presence.' For me, this means that the existence of God's love is so real that, even in the greatest moments of darkness, I can't give way to doubt. True, I'm unable to account for the darkness, but the smallest ray of light is enough to convince us that the sun is there, hidden behind the clouds. When I look at my life with the eyes of faith, I grasp the truth of St Paul's words, 'We know that in everything God works for good with those who love him' (Rom. 8:28).

Since the first Good Friday, death has ceased to have the last word! At the end of all our journeys lies an immense hope, standing out like a rainbow above our heads. That hope is Easter. It signifies promise, anticipation. No Christian may forget this message or keep it to himself. Certainly I've known suffering, but it has never held me back. The crucifixion was transformed into victory. So Calvary has become a very special place for us, where we can best understand the Apostle Paul's words on the wisdom of God, which men interpret as folly: 'Here are we preaching a crucified Christ; to the Jews an obstacle that they cannot overcome, to the pagans madness, but to those who have been called, whether Jews or Greeks, a Christ who is the power and the wisdom of God' (1 Cor. 1:23–24).

Pain is also often associated with illness, one of the visible signs of our steady journey towards the other life . . .

In a pastoral letter to our sick, I asked them to write and tell me how they understood their suffering and their illness. I received some moving replies. Nearly all those letters touched on the central problem of our human existence: the meaning of life. Quite a few of our invalids felt that illness was a process of purification. One young woman summed up her experience as follows:

Even when an illness begins to declare itself by certain early signs, we don't really believe that it will happen to us sooner or later. There's so much work to get through, looking after the children, the home, and so on. We make plans for the future. Life seems so beautiful that it claims our full attention. That was how I felt. But one day illness struck. I had to find new hope somewhere.

Another sick person wrote:

Of course I knew that today's traffic claims its victims. I, too, had read the accident statistics for public holidays. But I never believed that it would happen to me. One Monday morning I said goodbye to my wife as usual and went to work. Some hours later I woke up in a hospital bed. From now on, I thought, my life will be completely changed. The world, the future, daily cares, my work and my hobbies, my dreams and plans, all this will crumble to nothing. From that moment my existence was contained in the four walls of a hospital ward. Time, which had gone galloping by, seemed suddenly to stand still.

A third invalid explained:

When it happens you feel bitter, you don't accept it. You ask yourself, 'Why me?' Everything you've worked hard to build up suddenly comes crashing down. You feel helpless. One day follows another, full of grey mists and shadows. You feel sorry for yourself. And it isn't much comfort to think that others are even worse off.

Some of these experiences were strangely reminiscent of Job's lamentation in the Old Testament: 'Have I the strength to go on waiting? What use is life to me, when doomed to certain death? Is mine the strength of stone, or is my flesh bronze? Can any power be found within myself, has not all hope deserted me?' (Job 6: 11—13).

Willingly or otherwise, the sick person comes to ask himself the ultimate question that every existence must face: the question of the very meaning of our human adventure. A question so often suppressed by the hustle and bustle of everyday life, because our materialistic world never raises it. A question that demands an answer and a readiness to listen attentively.

So a half-answer isn't enough for a human being?

No. Otherwise I risk becoming closed in on myself, with no protection against existential anguish. So I must turn to the one who holds the key to life and death: God. When I discover him in the heart of my anguish, all that suffering takes on a new meaning. Then peace can descend. Then I speak to God in the words of the Psalmist, 'In my distress I called to Yahweh and to my God I cried' (Ps. 18:7). I begin a conversation with him. And perhaps it isn't immediately possible to say those words that revive an existence: 'Lord, what do you want me to do with my disabled life, with its so drastically reduced possibilities? With my wretched pains and my tormented body?' This question I ask the one who came to take upon himself all our human suffering: Jesus crucified. A wonderful Christian testimony can spring from the loneliness of illness, but only if I forget myself. Then the sick-room is no longer a prison cell, but a place where others can make a discovery: the discovery of a kind and gentle presence. At last I have the time to listen. I no longer feel empty. I can help someone!

I'm not trying to restore the value of suffering and illness by saying that they're blessings. But they can serve to reveal God's hidden presence to us. He who revealed himself in Christ is not an omnipotent, insensitive God, unmoved by pain. He's a God who shows himself to be weak and vulnerable, a God handed over to the mercy of men.

As for me, I always endeavour to accept suffering as an integral part of my Christian life, my spiritual journey. When pain rears its head – no matter what form it takes – I'm tempted to press on regardless, without letting it oppress me, without draining the cup to the last dregs. I'm not one of those people who welcome pain for its own sake. But at the same time, I feel that, in my suffering, God is challenging me to accept his message. That's precisely why I want to draw a lesson from it. Today the avoidance of suffering is too hastily justified on the grounds that otherwise it may bring discouragement, depression, neurasthenia. This would indeed be the case if one approached and endured suffering purely as a crude, isolated phenomenon. But when we recognize it as a mysterious encounter with the one who loves us, as a secret rendezvous with God, then we can also leave it to God to decide for himself when he wants our suffering to cease.

It's impressive to see how pain, acknowledged and accepted, can transform a soul. A person whose life had been one long agony once said to me with a cheerful smile, 'I've never really suffered.' When man surrenders to God, it isn't a void that extends before him but the fullness of God. All the saints tell us so: even as you empty yourself, you're opening yourself to God. That's why we have to enter into suffering as if we were entering a sanctuary, in a spirit of faith, silently worshipping God whose plans for us are mysterious, and not with an attitude of resignation to the inevitable.

You're approaching the end of your episcopal ministry. When you take stock of your life, what do you see as its most radiant moments?

Obviously, the most intense moments aren't on the surface of things, so it's difficult to point to this or that external fact or event. I would designate as moments of very deep joy the Pentecost Mass of 1977, which we celebrated in the Basilica of St Peter, in Rome, during the International Congress on Charismatic Renewal. Or again, my pilgrimage to Jerusalem on the occasion of my priestly jubilee. But I've experienced the most radiant moments of my life on encountering souls in whom I could see a reflection of God's face.

Whom have you in mind, for example?

It's always risky to cite the names of living people. And those I have in mind come from a variety of countries. But I'm thinking of such people as John XXIII, or Helder Camara, to cite only well-known names, for there are others.

May I ask you to give us your wholly personal creed?

For me to believe primarily means to open oneself to the

64

living God, made flesh in Jesus Christ. God is a personal mystery, God is love.

I'm a Catholic because I've found in my Church the fullness of God's love and truth. For me God is the Trinity.

As in the life of Jesus, Mary continues to be a mother in my own life. I see Mary as the one who brings God and men together.

When I look back on the seventy-five years of my life, I feel that I'm rereading an enthralling book. I discover a whole series of facts and events which had escaped my notice at the first reading. The French philosopher Gabriel Marcel once said, 'Life is like a sentence whose meaning cannot be grasped until the last word is uttered.' Today, as I skim through the book of my life, I can only thank God with deep emotion. At that moment I have to acknowledge that it was not I who chose him; it was he who called me by my name, took me by the hand and guided each of my steps. Day after day I've experienced his great love. For many a long year, he's always been close to me, faithful to me, despite my own resistance and my frequent refusal to match up to his grace.

What are your plans for the immediate future?

My work will be essentially ecumenical and charismatic. I intend to go on serving the renewal of the Church. I have many journeys already planned.

Do you intend to retire from public life eventually?

I have no such plans as long as I remain in good health. Even now, I can see new creative horizons opening up for me. Conferences and meetings in North and South America have already been scheduled for next year. My diary is relatively full until 1982. I think that by then I shall be ready to think gently about the 'last journey'.

And what do you hope to find at the end of that journey?

A new, magnificent world. If I had nothing to look forward to on leaving this world, life would have no meaning for me. I could understand neither sorrow nor true love. For it's only in the light of eternity that I can envisage these two realities. Surely there can be no such thing as absurd, motiveless suffering! Pain cannot be the last word. It can be understood only as the labour of childbirth. It's precisely because, in the last reckoning, our earthly life is simply a novitiate, a time of preparation for eternity, that, in spite of all the darkness, I see the ray of light which illuminates the events of my life and explains them in terms of love. I've always searched for that love, and I can understand it only as a requisite of eternity. It's an inspiring proof of the victory of life over death. The only future I'm awaiting is one that I see as light, brightness, joy and the fulfilment of everything that I've ardently desired on earth. As Léon Bloy lay dying, he was asked, 'What do you feel at this moment?' He replied, 'An enormous curiosity.' I hope that my answer will be, 'An immense confidence in the love of God.'

On retiring as Archbishop, I was asked to state, in a few words, my reasons for being a man of hope. Well, here are a few lines which I offer you as a résumé of my spiritual life and as my ultimate message:

The Christian is a man of hope,
because he knows
where he comes from,
where he is going.
He knows that he comes from God

and returns to Him,
to be immersed for ever
in the fullness of Life
of the Father, the Son and the Spirit,
in communion with the angels and the saints,
whose Queen is Mary.
He knows that he is called
to enter a new world
that no eye has seen,
no ear has heard,
no heart has conceived,
a world prepared by God
for those who love Him,
a world surpassing all hope.
May each one of us,
at the end of his earthly life,
sing with joy and gratitude
the moving antiphon of Advent,
'O Wisdom, you fill the universe
and hold all things together
with strength and sweetness.
O Come to teach us
the way of truth.'

PART TWO

7

Called to Hope

Cardinal, your words and actions are full of optimism and immense hope. From where do you draw this strength?

I'm a man of hope because I believe that with each new day God recreates the world. And so, where God is concerned, we must always be ready for the unexpected. Our lives are not governed by impersonal deterministic laws, nor are we wholly at the mercy of the gloomy forecasts of the sociologists. Always and everywhere God is close to us, unpredictable and loving. I'm an optimist because I believe that the Holy Spirit is God's creative spirit. With each new morning he gives those who welcome him renewed joy and hope. Who would venture to say that God's love and imagination can be exhausted? Hope is a duty, not a luxury. To hope doesn't mean to dream but to trust God.

I have to acknowledge in all sincerity that my life has been one long series of surprises from the Holy Spirit. Obviously, I too have known desperate situations. Since I'm only human, I'm often tempted to resign myself to the inevitable and say, 'there's no way out'. But it's precisely at those moments that, in a way no human mind can explain, I believe in the presence and power of the Holy Spirit. Many facts, encounters, events and circumstances have made me perceive the continuity of his action. And regardless of the apparent storms and upheavals, this assurance brings me an inner joy as certain as my own existence.

What happens in the course of a human life probably also applies to the life of the Church . . .

The history of the Church includes both sombre pages and eloquent testimonies to the wonders of the Holy Spirit. Just think how often, in desperate times, the saints have projected a radiant beam of light on the path of humanity!

And yet when you consider the way the world is going, it's often the negative things that seem to prevail: war, terrorism, suicide, contempt for human life, and so on.

The world is like a painting by Rembrandt: you have light and also shadows. Good and evil are inextricably interwoven. At the worst moments of the Church's history, saints suddenly loom out of the darkness, while the centuries which we regard as centuries of faith are shot through with shadows.

It's up to each Christian to be a light for the world and a sign of hope. The apostle Peter even said that a Christian must be able to account for his hope at every moment of his life. Doesn't this urge the Christian to examine his conscience? We're too ready to repeat the disappointed sigh of the disciples of Emmaus, 'We had hoped, but now . . .' (Luke 24:21). Hope is not to be confused with natural optimism. It doesn't in any way deny the reality of evil and sin in the world. But when the sun is hidden by fog, by clouds or the darkness of night, it doesn't mean that it has ceased to exist. A single ray of light is enough to make me believe in the sun, in a bright warm world. Far too many of our contemporaries live in fear and anguish. Their criticisms are negative and biased because, with downcast eyes, they can only contemplate the ground. No wonder they don't discover the stars shining above their heads!

And how can one help men to raise their eyes to the stars?

I would like to cry out to Christians of my generation, 'We need hope as we need our daily bread!' And to the many young people, too, who no longer believe in the future of the Church and set themselves against everything they call 'the institution', I want to say: 'The Church is turning to tomorrow and therefore to the young generation. By virtue of its mission, the Church is striving to create the future and hope.'

So Christians should carry hope before them like torchbearers lighting up the night?

Yes. God prepares for us things that no eye has ever contemplated and no human heart has ever anticipated, things that transcend all our dreams; because his love for us is inconceivable, it's greater than our hearts, our thoughts and our searching. God patiently adjusts himself to us. He walks beside us along the Jerusalem road to Emmaus. Instead of being distressed by the pessimistic words of his disciples, he has things to tell them which move them intensely and rescue them from their narrow outlook. Tirelessly, God makes them understand this: 'I keep my promise!' Ever since the first Good Friday death has ceased to have the last word. At the end of all our journeys lies an immense hope which stands out like a rainbow in the sky above us. That hope is Easter. It signifies promise and anticipation. No Christian may forget this message or keep it to himself. Called by the Master, he has to make his way to Jerusalem, and from there to Judaea, to Samaria, and to the heart of the five continents. We have to rediscover the true foundations of our hope. Life can spring only from those seeds that fall into the earth and die, trustfully surrendering themselves to the fertility of the soil and to the sun which marks the dawn of each day. In the same way, our Christian hope springs from the depths of suffering. It's rooted in suffering and draws its strength from it.

In Jesus, it's God himself who becomes the life-giving seed.

Yes, in his confrontation with evil, God reveals himself as the greatest power and also as the most powerful weakness. In Jesus, he grapples openly with evil. He clashes with it, he's martyrized, mortally wounded. And note that Jesus doesn't win the battle by suddenly drawing on his mighty power in order to save himself. He doesn't destroy evil simply by breathing on it. His victory relies on other means: he accepts us, together with our sins and our human distress. God loves us to his own cost. He pays a great price for loving us. So, you see, Jesus dies twice. First, in a spiritual way: 'My God, my God, why have you deserted me?' (Matt. 27:46); and then by giving up his spirit: 'Father, into your hands I commit my spirit' (Luke 23:46). Through this self-surrender he becomes the master who conquers evil, sin and death. He doesn't triumph over them by the power of his majesty and the splendour of his glory, but by the almightiness of his helplessness. The grain of wheat has died and fallen into the earth. Jesus applies to himself what he had said about death as the source of life.

You mean that in this way we discover the true face of God in his suffering?

Yes. This is the internal logic of the incarnation. A

person who hasn't yet been stricken in his inmost being by the suffering of a loved one, loves only superficially, not genuinely. In the same way, God, in Jesus, was shaken by all the evil that exists in the world; he took it upon himself to accomplish, through his incarnation, the mighty work of redemption. This weakness of God was already implicit in the risk of creating the world and man, for in some way God effaced himself so that man may be created as a free being, with all the consequences that freedom entails. Hölderlin says in one of his poems that, in creating man, God acted like the sea, which creates continents by receding from the land. God mysteriously effaces himself so that man may live. The knowledge of this entitles me to an optimism which transcends all the negative things this world may harbour.

8

For Tomorrow's Church

One of the topics most frequently discussed today is the democratization of the Church. But surely the Church is more than a democracy?

The important issue in the Church isn't so much the democratic principle as the principle of coresponsibility, which implies the existence of a community in the Holy Spirit. When coresponsibility is misunderstood and, furthermore, sets persons against each other, as often happens in party politics, for example, then it becomes a mere caricature of itself. The Christian who treats coresponsibility merely as a democratic principle risks reducing his vision of the Church to a single dimension, in other words, to a purely sociological approach.

To illustrate the principle of coresponsibility, I often resort to the analogy of a car being overhauled at the garage. Each little cog has to be checked and each part thoroughly tested. But if you've lost the ignition key, you can't even start the car!

Now, Vatican II gave the Church new structures, but even this isn't enough: the Church signifies fellowship with Jesus Christ in the Holy Spirit, a community in which our common prayer acts as the ignition key.

We were all deeply aware of the role of the Holy Spirit at the last Conclave. There were no party discussions, only moments of prayer, of communion in the will of God. Then we elected the Pope, guided by what we felt to be the will of God. That's another way of electing, which far transcends the rules of the democratic procedure.

It isn't unusual to meet Christians, or even unbelievers, who accept only the gospel, or rather a certain way of reading the gospel. They give their full assent to Jesus Christ, but reject the Church as a superfluous, indeed harmful, mediation.

If we want to discover the bond uniting Jesus to the Church and the Church to Jesus, let's begin by clearing up a misunderstanding: the Church regularly discussed by the press, or on radio and television, is the Church seen through its visible structures. Naturally, the Church is also a clearly definable sociological entity. It's an historical reality, with its ups and downs, its crises, its holiness and also its wretchedness. It's the Church such as men have made it, from Peter to John Paul II. It has its peak moments and its depressions. Saints have cast their light upon it during the darkest periods, and its most glorious moments have been tainted with human wretchedness and weakness. In this historical reality the light and the shadows would succeed one another, and at times they were interwoven. But such a purely historical or sociological view of the Church is distorted because it's incomplete.

The true Church is a visible reality, but also an invisible one. Its secret lies beyond its sociological and historical appearance. In *Lumen gentium*, Vatican II has given much prominence to these two aspects. That document presents the Church as an institutional and partly juridical reality, but also and mainly as a mystical, sacramental, spiritual reality. If a person doesn't accept this divine mystery and looks at the Church solely from the sociological angle, he may perhaps succeed in 'reforming' an aspect of the Church, but he isn't 'renewing' it. A Christian can't renounce the community of faith in the Holy Spirit with impunity. In this connection, let me quote the words of an Orthodox bishop, which admirably express the role of the Holy Spirit in the Church:

> Without the Holy Spirit, God is far away, Christ stays in the past, the Gospel is a dead letter, the Church is simply an organization, authority is a matter of domination, mission a matter of propaganda, the liturgy no more than an evocation, Christian living a slave morality. But in the Holy Spirit, the cosmos is resurrected and groans with the birth-pangs of the Kingdom, the risen Christ is there, the Gospel is the power of life, authority is a liberating service, mission is a Pentecost, the liturgy is both memorial and anticipation, human action is glorified. The Church shows forth the fellowship of the Trinity.

Now that is the Church as I see it with the eyes of faith, beginning with Jesus Christ who willed and founded it. That Church is the privileged place of Christ's presence, mysteriously and forever fulfilling within it what he began and lived through two thousand years ago.

Should the concept of 'the privileged place' be identified with 'no salvation outside the Church'?

Obviously, to believe in the Church as 'the privileged place' by no means implies that God doesn't also act outside its visible frontiers. We know that he sent his Son for the salvation of the world; for he wants the light of his grace to illuminate and warm all men of good will, whether or not they're aware of it. But we also know that when God establishes a privileged relationship with man – both personally and collectively – this involves a greater responsibility on man's part, a mission to hand on the message he's received. When man receives God's special love, he's required to give more.

In Mary we see the greatest manifestation of God's special love. But remember that at the same time he awakens in her a spiritual motherhood which extends to all mankind. It's in this sense that we call the Church the 'privileged place' of our encounter with God. In and through the Church, the Lord gives us his word, his life and his spirit in abundance.

So in this light the Church would be, so to speak, the home of God's word?

The New Testament hands on to us the history of Jesus: his life, his preaching, his suffering, his death and resurrection. But this history isn't over and done with. What the Lord proclaimed and lived doesn't belong solely to the past; Christ yesterday is also Christ today, our contemporary. The word of the one who prompted his listeners to say, 'No man has ever spoken like this one', didn't die with him. It still carries men along today, it sweeps through and beyond the centuries like a mysterious wave. Without the Church, we would never, in fact, have received this ever-living word, echoed for us by Scripture. For the Church has faithfully taken it up in the past and handed it down, from generation to generation, to the present day. Before printing was invented, Scripture was handed on for centuries by generations of scribes. Their illuminations are masterpieces of the Christian faith. Without this service of the Church, this fidelity to the text, we would have lost the word of God.

But the Church not only took care to hand on the treasure entrusted to it; from the earliest times, it distinguished the authentic inspired writings from an abundant apocryphal literature. It separated the wheat from the chaff and retained those books of Scripture which had captured the true, authentic message. From the beginning, the Church has watched over this treasure entrusted to its care: it has interpreted it, analysed it and enabled us to live it. At each eucharistic celebration, the Church invites us to participate in the meal of the Word before sharing the bread of life. Without the Church's living tradition, Scripture would be exposed to the arbitrary interpretations of all and sundry and to whatever reading happens to be fashionable at a given time. Tossed about by every wind that blows, we would have to navigate without chart and compass. Tradition and Scripture are one. Tradition gives us the word, while the word illuminates and guides tradition. Their reciprocal relation and influence are of vital importance.

This is how Vatican II expresses the relation between the Church welcoming the word and the word interpreted by the Church:

> The task of authentically interpreting the word of God, whether written or handed on, has been entrusted exclusively to the living teaching office of the Church, whose authority is exercised in the name of Jesus Christ. This teaching office is not above the word of God, but serves it, teaching only what has been handed on, listening to it devoutly, guarding it scrupulously, and explaining it faithfully by divine commission and with the help of the Holy Spirit; it draws from this one deposit of faith everything which it presents for belief as divinely revealed.

Scripture cannot be the word of God if we separate and isolate it from the Church, the bride and body of Christ. And the Church could not be the bride of Christ without having received the gift of discerning the word. These two phases in the coming of God to men are facets of the same mystery, different but intimately united facets.

Many people are still moved by Scripture, but see no point in approaching the sacraments.

We have to understand that Jesus' presence isn't confined to the thirty-three years of his life, for his action embraces all the centuries and will continue to do so until the end of time. He no longer acts through his physical presence, but in a mysterious, sacramental way. The Church Fathers have affirmed this time and again: it isn't the priest who baptizes, blesses, absolves, but Jesus Christ, acting in and through him. It's Jesus Christ who immerses us in the baptismal water in order to unite us to the mystery of his death and resurrection; it's Jesus who reconciles us with his Father, who stretches his hand over us to heal the sick in body and soul.

This action of Christ, who works through his Spirit, lies deep in the sacramental reality. Scripture tells us that when the sick woman touched his cloak, 'power emanated from him'. We aren't asked to encounter Jesus by an effort of the imagination which takes us back two thousand years. The Master is here at our door! He's knocking at our door and inviting himself to our table. The Church celebrates the Eucharist according to the Master's command, but the Eucharist, in its turn, forms the Church. To minimize the sacramental reality would be to affect the very heart of our faith and to imperil the future of our Christian life. We can never sufficiently meditate on the description of the first Christian community given in the Acts of the Apostles 2:42–46. That account is both exemplary and inspiring. For it tells us that the first Christians 'devoted themselves to the apostles' teaching and the brotherhood, to the breaking of bread and the prayers.'

9

Understanding
the Signs of the Times

Today we've reached an important turning-point in numerous areas of our life, and a great many things are in a state of upheaval. Bearing in mind this turmoil, how do you see the future of the Church?

To make out that future and delineate it for you, I would have to be a prophet, which I don't claim to be. But I think that, now we're reaching the end of the second millennium, we can already apprehend something: an evolution, in the sense of a search for authentic Christianity. Not so long ago, a journalist asked me, 'Would you say that today's Church is in a state of *revolution*, or of *evolution*?' I replied, '*Revolution* is too strong a word and *evolution* is too weak.' A true revolution in the Church is impossible for the simple reason that the Church would then have to disown itself. The word 'revolution' implies that you scrap everything that represents the old order and make a new departure, as in the case, for example, of the French or the Russian revolution.

Now the Church is true to itself precisely because its roots go deep into the past, as far down as the Old Testament of the patriarchs and the prophets. Today we still believe with the faith of Abraham. We've inherited a long history, now grievous, now glorious. We have our roots in the people of Israel, that people full of expectancy and hope. And historically Christ descends from that people, so do the apostles. We Christians are traditionalists by definition. In the life of the Church we live the past, the present and the future simultaneously: the Incarnation, the Resurrection and Pentecost are unique events and they're still continuing today. That's why it's impossible to speak of revolution in the Church. There are no sudden breaks in the history of the Church but only one continuous life.

How would you explain the fears, expressed even by some theologians, that the Church is dying?

A certain form of Church is dying, but another is being born. With Cardinal Marty, I say unhesitatingly, 'I'm more open to what is coming into being than to what is fading away.'

Not so long ago, a journalist wrote an article entitled *Is it Time to Reinvent the Church?*

My answer is: No, it's not for us to reinvent the Church. No one can do this better than our Lord Jesus Christ. What we have to reinvent is a fidelity, a more radical and contagious faith – and more love. No one blames us for being Christians. The only blame attached to us is that we're not Christian enough.

To penetrate more deeply into the mystery of the Church, we have to rediscover the source of unity; the Holy Spirit who, by his very nature, is the guardian, therefore also the supreme renovator. John the Evangelist says: 'When the Spirit of truth comes, he will lead you to the complete truth, since he will not be speaking as from himself, but will say only what he has learnt; and he will tell you of the things to come' (John 16:13). For he is the Spirit of Jesus and, step by step, he'll reveal to us what Jesus said to his disciples, things that today we still can't understand and bear.

And isn't it the very same Holy Spirit who's bringing the separated Churches together at this moment?

The same. In this case I see a clear sign of the times. It's absolutely essential for all Christians to acknowledge the full implications of Jesus' Testament, for only then can the world understand the Good News. Our divisions are barriers between the men of today and Christ.

It may be that in our ecumenical endeavours we aren't yet tuning in to each other on the 'long waves' – I mean the institutional ones – but we can already tune in to each other on the 'short waves' of our brotherly relations. In any case, I'm certain of one thing: the more we strive to resemble Christ, the more we hasten the hour of visible unity.

And what should be the distinctive traits of the Christian, in your view?

Scripture gives us the most reliable answer to your question, for it's asked explicitly and for the first time in the Acts of the Apostles. On the morning of Pentecost, Peter comes out of the Upper Room. Before him he sees a large crowd and he proclaims the Lord's death and resurrection. He declares that Joel's prophecy is being fulfilled and that the Spirit has descended on men. When Peter ends his first public speech, the crowd asks him, 'What must we do to become Christians?' Peter replies, 'You must repent, and every one of you must be baptized in the name of Jesus Christ for the forgiveness of sins, then you will receive the gift of the Holy Spirit' (Acts 2:38). From that moment, his words were to govern the whole history of the Church. They give us a precise definition of the Christian: the Christian is he who is converted to God, who through baptism is brought into the mystery of Christ's death and resurrection, who personally adheres to the Lord, and who opens himself to the action of the Holy Spirit.

You mean that every true Christian has undergone this conversion?

Yes. If we want to be authentic Christians, we have to change our way of life, we have to cast off the old self and our purely human wisdom. This stripping of self is the prerequisite of man's openness to Jesus Christ and his reception of the Holy Spirit.

To opt for Christ means to discover his face, to hear his voice, until we too can say in our turn, 'No man has ever spoken like this one' (John 7:46).

The importance of this personal encounter can never be sufficiently emphasized. For, all too often, Christians look upon Christianity as a mere ideology, a set of values, a moral code.

I once asked the great German theologian Karl Rahner, 'Why is it that Catholics are reticent when the conversation turns to Mary?' I was struck by his answer: 'One of the reasons', he said, 'is that all too often they regard Christianity as an abstraction. And abstractions don't need a mother.' No, Jesus is not an abstraction, Christianity is not an intellectual vision. Christ is present, living in the heart of each generation, for the past two thousand years. And living in an even truer sense than we do ourselves. His mysterious presence is constantly with us.

Faith seems to have become so difficult in our time!

The object of our faith is not primarily a dogma, a rite, a moral rule, but Jesus Christ. Dogmas, rites, rules are no more than the visible expression of man's relationship with God and of God's relationship with man. Our faith must help us to discover in Jesus Christ the person of the living God. We too must be able to say what Paul Claudel said, on the eve of his conversion one Christmas day, as he stood in Notre Dame Cathedral: 'Lord, all of a sudden you've become a real Person for me!' The discovery of Jesus Christ as Saviour must determine and transform our lives.

10

Dialogue with the World

Today everyone's using the word 'dialogue'. What do you expect from a dialogue between the Church and the world?

Listening to men means living, with them, the situation of today's world or, as the Council says, 'discerning the signs of the times'. To listen means to understand, to judge and to distinguish the eternal values from transient things. To listen means to separate the liberating truth from what might lead us to a new slavery. In short, to listen to our time means to analyse critically yet with kindness. Here there's no contradiction, for the gift of listening postulates this type of concentration. The world with which the Church wants to hold a dialogue is the whole human family: the Church must live its anxieties and share its hopes with all men and light the way for them.

What major changes do you notice today?

The first basic fact that holds my attention is the enormous upsurge of science and technology. These offer man, provided that he applies them intelligently, undreamt of possibilities and hopes regarding the liberation of matter. Men are gaining an increasingly keen awareness of their solidarity and interdependence. In a world where geographical distances are no longer obstacles, where I can fly from Brussels to Bombay in just a few

87

hours, we're witnessing unprecedented advances. The technology of communication – the press, radio, television, the cinema – is bringing us closer and closer to each other. Human problems no longer arise simply at regional or national level; they call for intercontinental solutions. Tomorrow they may take on interplanetary dimensions. Recently a European statesman very pertinently remarked that, today, any problem that isn't posed in a world perspective is a wrongly worded problem.

Scientific and political barriers are being crossed because of the urgent need to internationalize the political life of the nations. Today men are overcoming ethnological and cultural distances and we're beholding an unprecedented encounter between the peoples of the world.

In a human society fast growing to world dimensions, we can no longer be closed in on ourselves and exclude others. We must apply to this great human family what St Paul demands of every Christian: 'If one member suffers, all suffer together; if one member is honoured, all rejoice together' (1 Cor. 12:26).

The development of modern technology has yet another consequence: the efforts to unify our planet have enabled the Third World to awaken. This collective consciousness of the poor, who represent the vast majority of mankind, is perhaps the decisive event of our time. In this way the proletarian revolution, which marked the history of the West in the latter half of the nineteenth century, is becoming established at world level.

History may well have its own logic, but this doesn't exclude man's personal freedom and responsibility.

At one and the same time we're being incorporated into

history and helping to make history. In other words, these far-reaching, radical changes can be to our benefit or turn against us. Ultimately, the liberating power of technology lies in the hands of man. The misuse of this all-powerful technology could dehumanize society and abolish all respect for life.

The same is true of the unification of our planet. The evergrowing contacts between peoples or cultures can just as easily impoverish mankind as enrich it. It would be a great loss for humanity if it repressed its creative freedom because of its desire to be one family.

In the last analysis, the awakening of the Third World is the pivot around which everything else will revolve. This awakening can lead to either the suicide or the resurrection of the Western world. The entry of the developing countries into the historical process concerns each one of us. We have to hear the cries of suffering of the countless poor people who are hungering and thirsting for more justice.

The time has come to put an end to fruitless, costly discussions and to start building up a new, more human world, founded on truth, love and freedom, as John XXIII put it so clearly in his encyclical *Pacem in Terris*. We can no longer resign ourselves to the fact that two-thirds of the human race are living below the poverty line and are therefore suffering in their very flesh because of the terrifyingly unequal distribution of this world's goods. Civilization is unworthy of its name if it goes on indulging in this collective and social sin. It's essential for us to get down to the roots of this evil and to do our utmost so that the individual and all mankind may live in the hope of a better future. Every moment counts! In a world where a human being is born every second, we have no right to defer the problem by a single second. Dire poverty destroys and waits for no man.

You would say, then, that the major task of our century is to foster a concern for man?

This is a task that no one has the right to neglect, and least of all the Christian. What today's world needs most, and is entitled to demand of us Christians, is a growth of spiritual values which give life, suffering and death their true meaning.

Today's world is more than ever in search of its soul. I'm thinking now of the rediscovery of prayer. Everywhere we see the young seeking for something transcendental. Some young people are travelling even to the Far East in search of their souls. Isn't it tragic that they're searching way out there for something that we should have given them as their birthright: the very wealth of the gospel message?

The world is hungering for God, and many are dying without ever having known the Saviour.

We Christians must give the world what St Paul designates as the fruits of the Spirit: love, joy, peace, patience, kindness, goodness, cheerfulness, politeness, self-control. Basically, it's a matter of forming a new and less selfish human race, conscious of its solidarity and collective responsibility. This is primarily a spiritual and moral task.

Considered from this angle, isn't the Gospel ever-topical precisely because it excludes no one?

Yes, indeed. Christianity isn't tied to any particular culture. It can make all cultures fertile. The universality of Christianity is a treasure for all mankind. Today we have to make our souls grow to the dimensions of universality.

90

And how can the Christian avoid being content with a vague, passive feeling of sympathy for the whole world?

The fact of seeing Christ in our brother must be the mainspring and moving spirit of our actions. It represents the existential truth of Christianity. As St John puts it, 'He who does not love his brother whom he can see, cannot love God whom he has not seen' (1 John 4:20); and again, 'If any one has the world's goods and sees his brother in need, yet closes his heart against him, how does God's love abide in him? Little children, let us not love in word or speech but in deed and in truth' (1 John 3:17–18).

Sadly, many baptized people reduce Christian living to a few isolated religious practices and forget all about justice and love of neighbour. Yet Christ came to vivify all the dimensions of human life. One of the great achievements of our time is a keen, growing awareness that Christ is not only the life of the soul, but also the life of the body. Christ is concerned with every aspect of man.

To reduce Christian living to a few pious exercises – however important these may be – is a distortion of Christianity. It's a betrayal of the Christian faith. Our concern for eternal blessings can never be an excuse for evading temporal problems. A Christian who takes refuge in the thought of heaven and lets his brother suffer from hunger is wounding Christ himself. Our eschatological hope cannot be an excuse for shirking our duties. We have to work as long as we still have time to fulfil them.

A Christian can't limit his Christianity to attendance at Sunday Mass. In any case, no Christian can be satisfied with a negative morality consisting of prohibitions.

11

Towards Full Unity

When the ecumenical movement was really set in motion during the sixties, there were some spectacular moments, such as the meetings of Paul VI and Patriarch Athenagoras in Jerusalem, Istanbul and Rome. The press described them as world events. But since then, the mass media have had little to say about the great events of ecumenism. How do you account for this?

Remember that meanwhile some three hundred documents, exchanged over the last ten years between Rome and Constantinople, have been published under the title *Tomos Agapis*, that is, the Book of Brotherly Love. The mass media didn't highlight the event because it occurred at a level that escaped their attention. We can hope that the ecumenical movement – which has already proved itself irreversible – will make giant strides towards the restoration of full, visible Christian unity. Each effort to harmonize that essential unity with the legitimate diversity of the Christian confessions is already in itself an ecumenical achievement, a furthering of our fellowship in the Holy Spirit.

Yet one sometimes has the impression that ecumenism is still confined to a circle of experts.

That's why it's all the more essential that the efforts to restore the unity of the people of God be made at all levels. Active ecumenism must be the constant concern of all Christians, whether or not they are theologians. The grievous experience of the Council of Florence in the fifteenth century must never be repeated: on that occasion, unity between the Catholic and Orthodox Churches was re-established by their respective hierarchies, but the ordinary people weren't prepared for it, and although the union was already ratified, it died at birth.

But, I repeat, I have great confidence in the future.

Do you think that we'll achieve Christian unity by the end of this century?

Obviously, I don't know precisely when it will happen. I think that Christians of my generation will see only the horizon of the 'Promised Land', like Moses. Judging by the signs of the times, the day of visible Christian unity is drawing nearer. The star which led the wise men to Bethlehem is already shining in the sky of unity. The pilgrims of unity have already set out. Theirs is a stony path and its trail is often lost in the wilderness. But, unlike the wise men from the East, our pilgrims bear well-known names: Paul VI, John Paul II, Ramsey and Coggan, Athenagoras. . . . They're journeying towards the Bethlehem of unity, and many times they've encountered each other on the way. Each is bringing treasures from his own land. The Church of Peter is bringing the gold of its traditional unity. The Church of John is bringing the incense of its mystical and spiritual tradition. The Church of Paul is carrying the holy and prophetic books. And so they make their way. Often the star above them stops shining and they have to take their bearings anew. But there's every sign that they're drawing nearer to Bethlehem. May they, too, find the mother and child there. It's difficult to imagine disunited children coming home without their mother waiting for them at the door to lead them to the Lord. What the wise men discovered on entering the cave was not the God they had expected to see. They beheld a child who confounded their calculations, their hypotheses, but at the same time surpassed all their hopes: the Emmanuel was lying in a cradle, a poor child, wrapped in swaddling clothes. I don't know when and how this return to Bethlehem will take place. Perhaps at a new Council, at some joint rendezvous in Jerusalem's Upper Room.

And surely model communities like the Ecumenical Centre of Ottmaring, near Augsburg, or the Abbey of Taizé are also signposts on the road to Bethlehem?

Certainly they are. Ottmaring is important. Taizé is important. The only difference lies in their respective vocations. In Ottmaring I find the convincing example of a true community life shared by Christians. I've already visited the Centre twice, and each time I was immediately convinced of that prophetic reality, which I see as an anticipation of fully restored unity; for at Ottmaring everyone endeavours to make possible through love what we can't yet achieve on a larger scale.

And Taizé is also making a considerable contribution to Christian unity through its radiant example. There, as in Ottmaring, you find men working passionately for the unity of the Churches, yet without abandoning their own tradition.

Recently, I was reading in my breviary a phrase which is very applicable to these ecumenical centres: 'Draw close to God together, then shall the shadows depart from your faces.'

I believe that in these many ways we're advancing towards a future full of hope. Max Thurian, the theologian of Taizé, echoes this hope when he writes:

94

Has not the time come for each Christian and each Church to rediscover the true significance of the ministry of the Bishop of Rome, the servant of the servants of God, as the pastor at the service of the apostolic faith, the unity of the Church and peace for all? How much longer can we go on spurning this sign of unity without constantly succumbing to a fragmentation far removed from a fruitful plurality in unity? We are beginning to dream of the day when, despite all the obstacles within institutions – I do not mean the institution of Christ which hands on the Gospel – the leaders will exercise their authority with a view to recognizing in the Church of Christ all those who, following their own paths, have never ceased to hold in common what is essential and fundamental. Here is the sign which Our Lord himself has given us: 'Be one, so that the world may believe.'

12

God's Today

The fascinating figure of Jesus dominates the horizon of history.
For two thousand years it's held the attention of mankind. Isn't
it also attracting countless young people today, and rather
unexpectedly?

Yes, our young people are asking us what the Greek
pilgrims in Palestine once requested of the apostle Philip:
'Sir, we should like to see Jesus' (John 12:21). They
would like to encounter him in our personal witness, to
read him on our faces and hear him in our voices. Proclaiming the truth of Christianity also means giving
proof that Christ continues his life in us and wants it to
blossom fully in us.

Yet it seems that, for many of our contemporaries, it's man rather
than Jesus who is central to this quest.

I think that we must tell the world, as John Paul II has
done in his first encyclical, that what we discover in
Jesus *is* man – yes, man himself. There have been many
tendencies to minimize the Saviour's humanity, but the
Church, for its part, has ceaselessly stressed that Jesus
Christ is truly man, endowed with a completely human
freedom. So we can't confuse the mystery of the incarnation with a mere appearance of God, a momentary
theophany in which God would have assumed a human
form in order to speak to men.

96

I think that, so far, we haven't sufficiently understood how human Jesus is, human to the point of feeling anguish at the thought of death, human to the point of crying out in utter despair on the cross. Unconsciously, we still make too sharp a distinction between his divinity and his humanity, as if they were two conflicting realities, as if Jesus were human despite his divinity, whereas he's fully human precisely by reason of his divinity.

Each page of the gospel tells us of the humanity of Christ: like other men, he's hungry and thirsty (Matt. 4.2: John 4:7; 9: 28). He's tired (John 4:6). He makes friends. He weeps over Lazarus (John 11:35). He feels sorry for the crowd (Matt. 15:32). His Father's love fills him with joy. He goes out to meet people with great simplicity and a sense of authority: the sinners, the sick, people suffering in mind and body, find understanding in him; and the seekers, hearing his call, are transformed by it. At each moment he carries out the mission entrusted to him by his Father, from the time of his temptation in the wilderness to his final decision in the Garden of Olives. He knows the human depths of suffering as well as union with the Father's will. Though a Jew, he unhesitatingly voices his objections to the Law when it stands in the way of love of neighbour.

Only in him can we understand ourselves and all our basic problems. Admittedly, he didn't come to resolve our scientific or technological problems. He came to give an answer to the most fundamental question of all: What is man? Why do we exist? Why do we suffer? What awaits us after death? Such questions are valid for all times and for every generation.

Robert Kennedy once said that the tragedy of young people in America is that everything is offered to them except the answer to the most fundamental question of all: 'Why do I exist?' In Jesus we find the ultimate motivation behind life, suffering and death. Without him, our existence is meaningless. Not only does he show us the way, but he walks beside us, he lives with us and in us. Jesus is the cause of our joy. Without him, we don't know ourselves. Pascal says that only in Jesus Christ do we know both God and ourselves.

Yet many of our contemporaries are asking themselves if Jesus Christ is truly the Son of God, in the strict, unequivocal sense.

This is an essential question, for the truth of our faith and the fate of Christianity depend on the answer. In 325 the first Ecumenical Council of Nicaea defined Jesus' divinity as an article of faith. The Council of Ephesus reiterated this proclamation of faith in 431 and, on the same occasion, stressed the human nature of Christ. Then in 451 we have the Council of Chalcedon proclaiming the unity of the two natures of Christ and clearly stating that he is truly man.

These Councils will forever remain the pillars of the temple of our faith. I dare say that these definitions could be worded with greater precision or more nuances, but their content cannot be modified with impunity. The divinity of Jesus Christ implies that in him were manifested the infinite riches, the unending fullnes of God's life and merciful love. He is Emmanuel, God with us. In him we discover the presence of the One who said of himself, 'I am the first, I am also the last' (Isa. 48:12), and again, 'I am with you always; yes, to the end of time' (Matt. 28:20). What we have here is an alliance. In Jesus this alliance assumes a new form of incomparable depth.

In him the living God offers men true life. In him God weaves himself into the fabric of our human history. The coming of Jesus gives the world a new, undreamt of meaning and brings it permanent light and hope. To recognize his divinity is to encounter in him the infinite transcendence of God's love. For Christians this encounter is a reality that quenches man's thirst for the infinite, wipes away all tears, heals all wounds. It's a source of life, peace, joy and trust. It helps each man to transcend the obstacles of hatred, war and death, and to attain to the ultimate hope.

Jesus' message is mainly about God, the Father who remains close to all men. His deeds and his mission demonstrate that with God, our Father, he has a relationship comparable to no other. And, finally, whereas his death on the cross had destroyed the hopes of his disciples and apparently justified his enemies, his resurrection shook the foundations of everything. For if God raised Jesus of Nazareth to life, although the leaders of the people had condemned him as a blasphemer, it means that his mission was authentic, that the Father's entire revelation was made through this man.

If Jesus of Nazareth were not God, the only Son of the Father, but simply the greatest of the prophets, God would have sent us a liberator from outside himself, but he wouldn't have committed himself, from the depths of his own being, to mankind's salvation. He would have remained for us the ever remote and inaccessible God, the unmoving prime mover of Aristotle. He would be the God of deism, that abstract, silent God whom the 'Death of God' theologians have brought to trial. But if Jesus is God, God from God, then we discover how true and passionate is God's love for us. We stand before a God who wants to share our destiny, our life and our death. We can say with John the Evangelist, and with the same joy, 'We ourselves have known and put our faith in God's love for us. . . . We love, then, because he loved us first' (1 John 4:16, 19).

In fact, the events of Christ's life, and more particularly his

99

death and resurrection, concern not only the Christian's personal life, but also the cosmic dimensions of life in Christ. . . .

Christ's whole life is an event that casts its radiance on each man. Of course, our faith in the risen Christ takes us beyond the world of the senses. The first witnesses saw this faith confirmed in their everyday experience: by reason of Jesus' resurrection, they became new men; a new Israel was created; a new order emerged. The eternally living Christ is the new Adam (1 Cor, 15:45), the new foundation of humanity.

Man receives life when he opens himself to this source, which is Christ. If, on the other hand, he trusts no one but himself, he becomes stunted. Jesus teaches us to open ourselves to God, to welcome him and to surrender ourselves to his love.

Paul goes so far as to say that 'God raised us up with Christ to enthrone us with him in heaven' (Eph. 2:6). The person of Jesus is the meeting-point of heaven and earth. In him, God wants to establish a new, personal relationship with each man. In his Letter to the Colossians, the Apostle of the Nations writes, 'For God wanted to be fully present in his son' (Col. 1:19).

Christ is the centre of creation, the peak of humanity. Human nature is God's language inscribed in time. God said, 'Let us make man in our own image' (Gen. 1:26). And Jesus Christ is that perfect image. Through his life, he disclosed the secret and the goal of God's creation.

Jesus teaches us in his own prayer, the Our Father, that we must speak to the Father when we pray. But the image of the father is undergoing a crisis: our contemporaries are even talking about a 'fatherless society'. . . .

No one can speak of the Father but Jesus himself. No one but the Son of God knows God. No one but the

Father knows the Son of God. Christ alone can reveal to us the mystery of the Father. When we say that God is our Father, we never quite capture the gentleness with which Jesus would use this word. The Hebrew word 'Abba' expresses all the trust of a child saying 'daddy'. That fatherhood also contains a tenderness which is somehow suggestive of the motherhood of God.

When we speak to God and call him 'Father', we can't limit this word to its purely masculine significance. God the Father also has the gentleness of a mother. Besides, Scripture says, 'Does a woman forget her baby at the breast? I will never forget you' (Isa. 49:15). Jesus himself promises his disciples who are willing to leave their home, their father and mother, brothers and sisters, that they will be repaid a hundred times over in both this world and the next (Matt. 19:29). God, who created love, contains within himself all the diversity of human love: the love of a father, a mother, a brother, a sister, the love of a husband, a wife, the sensitive understanding of a friend. All these human forms are condensed in God's fatherly love. And it's precisely because he loves us in this way that St Francis of Sales confidently affirmed, 'On the last day I would prefer to be judged by God than by my own mother.'

If we want to gain a deeper understanding of the Father's heart, we have to listen to Jesus; for he came to disclose the Father's secret to us. In this he was an incomparable master. Jesus has left us no learned books. He chose another way of explaining the Father's profound psychology to us. He told a story, probably the most moving of all the gospel stories: the parable of the prodigal son. What Jesus stresses in this parable isn't so much the image of the son as that of the Father. In doing so, he gives us a portrait of his own Father: the son is still a long way from home, but the Father already recognizes him from afar, because he's never ceased waiting for him. His heart goes out to meet his son. That's why he doesn't just stand there at the door but rushes out to greet the boy. He clasps him in his arms and kisses him, saying, 'My son was dead and he has come to life, he was lost and now I have found him.' And the family prepares a joyful feast (Luke 15:24). The father doesn't even give his son time to give suitable expression to his repentance. In this parable each word of Luke reveals God's fatherhood. The elder son resents this generosity. He thinks that his father is behaving emotionally and even unjustly. But God has his own manner of retribution. Here he shows a predilection for the poor, for those who have strayed, the prodigal sons. And we're all prodigal sons more or less!

Yet, from the human point of view, it's often difficult to believe in this very special love of the Father for each individual.

Yes, God's fatherhood does indeed surpass our human understanding. We feel lost in the infinity of this world with its four billion inhabitants. How can God possibly notice me in such a vast crowd? For me, it's comforting to know that in the Father's eyes I'm not just a drop in the ocean, a grain of sand in the desert, but his child, and that he has called me by my name. In his love he gives his full attention to each person. He doesn't get our names mixed up. He knows the history of each life, page by page, chapter by chapter. He even knows what's written between the lines and what remains implicit in the text. The Gospel gives us many proofs of this intimate knowledge. When Jesus encounters Nathanael, he says to him, 'I saw you under the fig tree' (John 1:48). Why had Nathanael attracted his attention? We don't know. Perhaps he was praying. But in any case, Jesus had noticed him and this is what matters.

Then again, on the eve of the Passover, the apostles

ask Jesus, 'Where would you like us to prepare for your Passover supper?' He replies, 'Go to a certain man in the city and tell him, "The Master says, my time is near; I am to keep Passover with my disciples at your house"' (Matt. 26:17–18).

Once we're wholly convinced that God's loving concern extends to such details, our life is changed. In his *Memorial*, Pascal makes God say, 'This particular drop of my blood I shed for you.' But God did more than that. He shed all his blood for each one of us. We can't measure God by means of our mathematical calculations. His gift to each one of us is complete, total. In his eyes, each one of us has a particular vocation, quite distinct from that of his neighbour. God, the Father, loves us. He cares about each one of us, nothing escapes the fullness of his attention, the abundance of his love, of his gifts, however unaccountable this may be.

How do you explain that this fullness – the gifts of the Holy Spirit, which were so visible in the early Church – seems to have faded away subsequently, only to reappear gradually and as late as today?

There have always been charismatic manifestations in the Church, but subsequent to the splendour of their presence in the early Church, they became more discreet. You find them in the lives of the saints and in the mystical tradition of the Eastern Churches.

So today God is summoning us with the words: 'Listen even more attentively to what the Spirit has to say to you'?

Precisely. And so that we may do his will even more faithfully. Jesus says, 'If you, then, who are evil, know how to give your children what is good, how much more will the heavenly Father give the Holy Spirit to those who ask him!' (Luke 11:13). Isn't this God's supreme gift? At times we tend to think that God is silent. But, in fact, we don't hear his voice because there's too much noise, too much disturbance in us. God can be reached only on certain wave-lengths. The Council, which spoke of the signs of the times, pointed out to us that we must open ourselves from the heart to the Spirit who is summoning us today. Georges Bernanos admirably defines this call of the Spirit when he says, 'It is God who is expecting of us what men expect of us.'

In the canon of the Mass we ask God that 'we who are nourished by the body and blood of Christ may be filled with his Holy Spirit and become one body'. We can't receive this gift of unity unless we forget ourselves and become positively attentive to others. Why shouldn't we pray to the Holy Spirit daily to grant us this gift?

Our awareness of being the body of Christ should urge us, then, to acknowledge each other as brothers in the community of God's children?

Yes, this is certainly what the Holy Spirit requires most of today's Christians. The second chapter of the Acts of the Apostles gives us a description of that brotherly community, which is as topical as ever. The first Christians met regularly to hear the teaching of the apostles, to celebrate the Eucharist and to pray together.

As soon as Peter was released from prison, he made straight for the Christian community. If we want to be true Christians, we have to be an apostolic, brotherly, eucharistic and praying community. We need to be all these things to welcome the word of God together, to remain in continuity with our tradition. Such a community is a touchstone, a support, an aid. It frees us from our inhibitions, our hesitations.

104

How would you account for the tensions, apparent throughout the centuries, between the charismatic Church and the institutional Church, given that the Holy Spirit vivifies the whole Church?

The Holy Spirit acts along sacramental lines but, at the same time, he works in an original fashion along charismatic lines. When the Spirit breathes anew, difficulties arise until his breath has become integrated into the very life of the Church. Just think, for example, of the foundation of new religious orders: the Franciscans, the Dominicans, the Jesuits. . . . In their early days these foundations often had their moments of tension. Such situations can best be compared to the labour of childbirth. Bringing a child into the world involves pain.

An old canonist in Rome used to say to us, 'Release the floods, we canonists will channel their course for you!' It takes time for the visible and the invisible Church, the institutional and the charismatic, to blend harmoniously. Of course momentary tensions can arise!

You would say, then, that the invisible, charismatic Church must be sustained by the visible, institutional Church?

We're not dealing with two separate Churches confronting each other, but with one single Church having a twofold dimension. Think of the bark of a tree: it supports the sap but, at the same time, it's nourished by the sap.

Today there's a strong tendency to distinguish between charismatic Christians and socially or politically committed Christians. Doesn't such a distinction encourage polarizations?

I must tell you plainly that there are no charismatic Christians as opposed to non-charismatic Christians. This false distinction is as foolish as the assertion that

105

on the one hand there are baptized Christians and, on the other, non-baptized Christians. We're all charismatic Christians, in other words, we've all received the Holy Spirit. Let me illustrate what I mean. The Jesuits are known as the Society of Jesus. No one would conclude from this that we don't equally belong to the society of Jesus. It's simply that the generic term sometimes expresses a more definite aim. Similarly, no one has ever heard of Christians who aren't social. There's no question here of opting for one or the other, because the one completes the other.

The 'spiritual' Christian is right to give grace and prayer precedence over the activism and the naturalism that surround him. We can't save the world unless we're tuned in to God. When Jesus left his apostles, he didn't say, 'Now rush out to the world!' He told them to wait for the coming of the Holy Spirit in the 'upper room' of the Cenacle, in silence and prayer, with Mary. This they had to do first, before any of the subsequent events could occur.

But, at the same time, we have to acknowledge that all our talents are given to us to serve mankind. So we must come out of the 'upper room', as Peter did on the morning of Pentecost. For this is what we're called to do: we have to bring each man the Gospel in all its dimensions; to love God and bring others to love him. We have to translate our love into deeds! We can't just steep ourselves in Christian spirituality without, at the same time, participating in social and political tasks. The 'social' Christian is right to lay emphasis on the world's needs, the hardships of the poor, human wretchedness. But it would be wrong of him to forget that we need the Spirit to renew the face of the earth. We need his power and his charisms in order to help others, with determination and courage, to hear the word of God in this world.

So these two aspects, the charismatic and the social, are like the two sides of one coin?

Yes. The 'charismatic' Christian stresses the fact that God lives in him and with him. The 'socially committed' Christian stresses the fact that God lives in his neighbour. But his social involvement must have its roots in faith. If we want to be well-balanced Christians, we need to harmonize prayer with social commitment. We have a twofold mission. Christ didn't come to create a purely earthly paradise. For, as he says himself, 'My kingdom is not of this world' (John 18:36). Humanity's material well-being is not the ultimate goal of social action. Consequently, the spreading of the gospel can't be deferred until the social circumstances are more favourable for mankind. Holy Scripture tells us plainly that 'the Good News is proclaimed to the poor' (Matt. 11:5). Obviously, I realize that when a house is on fire, it isn't the right moment to start preaching the gospel. In this instance, water has absolute priority. But starving men have to be given both the means of living and reasons for living. We must offer them both. The Christ who refuses to change stones into loaves, and who says that man does not live on bread alone but on every word that comes from the mouth of God, is the same Christ who feeds the crowd in the wilderness. We must give men bread and the Eucharist. We must teach them both the alphabet and the catechism. We must give them social security and, at the same time, awaken their faith in God's providence. We have to save man's soul as well as his body. At one and the same time, we need social pioneers and saints.

As you've already pointed out, prayer is an important gift of the Holy Spirit for our time. I feel that, in the last analysis, prayer is also the 'secret of your success'.

107

For me, prayer means opening the soul and shutting out the 'atmospheric disturbances'. This implies silence and receptiveness. Prayer does not mean acquainting God with the facts, trying to make him attentive to our needs. Prayer signifies being receptive to the grace that God wants to give me. To pray is to let ourselves be guided by the Father's will, so that our whole life – from the search for daily bread to the transformation of the world – may be permeated with his love. Prayer means exposing ourselves to the love of the Father, in order to live more perfectly, as his sons, and in the wake of the Lord Jesus.

The first Book of Kings describes God's relationship with the prophet Elijah on Mount Horeb:

> The prophet was told, 'Go out and stand on the mountain before Yahweh'. Then Yahweh himself went by. There came a mighty wind, so strong that it tore the mountains and shattered the rocks before Yahweh. But Yahweh was not in the wind. After the wind came an earthquake. But Yahweh was not in the earthquake. After the earthquake came a fire, and after the fire the sound of a gentle breeze. When Elijah heard this, he covered his head with his cloak and went out and stood at the entrance of the cave. Then a voice came to him . . . (1 Kings 19:11–13).

God was not in the earthquake, not in the fire, not in the mighty wind, but in the sound of the gentle breeze.

That's the way God encounters men. And that's why we must be vigilant if we want to hear his voice.

More and more Christians are feeling an urgent need to pray. Prayer groups are springing up all over the world, and this is certainly more than a passing fashion.

They're showing the world that praise and worship are

108

once again becoming an integral part of the Christian life. Certainly, this is due to the promptings of the Holy Spirit, and in it I see one of the surest signs of hope for our time.

And what should we do when God doesn't appear to answer our prayers?

Even when God doesn't grant us what we ask of him, his answer is always the best one; for he loves us more than we love ourselves. Let me remind you of a significant episode in the life of St Augustine. His mother, Monica, spends a whole night praying in a little chapel on the African coast. She entreats God to prevent her son from leaving Africa for Rome, the city of corruption. And what happens? You have Augustine taking advantage of his mother's absence to steal away, board a ship, and set sail for Italy. Who would venture to say that God didn't answer Monica's prayer? But by doing the very opposite of what she was asking of him. God moved heaven and earth to answer her prayer, but in a totally different way. God wanted Augustine to go to Rome, and thence to Milan. For it was in Milan that he met St Ambrose, found the faith and became one of the greatest doctors of the Church.

Let us always remember that divine providence accompanies us, in its wisdom, from the beginning to the end of our lives. When we contemplate our lives with the eyes of faith, we also recognize signs of God's hidden presence in apparently fortuitous episodes. A few clues suffice to reveal a presence: when I come upon a matchstick in the desert or footsteps in the snow, I know that a man must have passed that way. Similarly, I recognize God's existence in my life thanks to various indications which faith reveals to me increasingly.

Sometimes God's attentive love can be seen in his very

choice of the hour and place of a man's death. No details are too trifling for God. I'm thinking of the death of Teilhard de Chardin, for instance, who was so alive to the significance of Easter. His books speak constantly of faith in the resurrection. Well, he died in New York on an Easter Sunday. I'm also thinking of Odo Casel, the liturgist. He toiled for twenty years to restore the living beauty of the Easter liturgy. He died in a Benedictine monastery during the Easter Vigil, just as the deacon was singing the paschal *Exultet*.

Cardinal, the disciples asked Jesus, 'Lord, teach us to pray.' What is the content of your prayer?

Here's a prayer which I composed one day, and which helps me to enter into the Lord's intimate presence:

> Give us, oh Lord,
> eyes for seeing,
> a heart for loving,
> breath for living.
>
> Give us eyes for seeing,
>
> give us, we beg, your eyes,
> to see through them
> the world and all mankind,
> to see their history and our own
> as you see them.
> Grant us to think your thoughts
> day by day,
> hour by hour.
> Help us gradually to become
> that for which you created us;
> let us adopt your view of things,
> your way of seeing things.

110

Make us responsive to your Word
which can enlighten and transform
the life of each of us.

Give us a heart for loving,

a heart of flesh and not of stone
for loving God and Man.
Give us, we beg, your heart,
that we forget ourselves
in perfect love.
We need to exchange our heart for yours,
our heart so slow
to love all others but ourselves.
Let it be you, oh Lord,
who loves through us.
Give us a heart to love Our Father,
to love Mary our Mother
and to love your brothers
who are also ours;
to love even in this world
those who have gone before us in the next –
to love also those
who walk beside us
here on earth
and who sometimes
are more difficult to love.

Give us the breath of life

that our lungs be constantly filled
with life-saving breath and air
to help us walk towards tomorrow
without a backward look or thought or effort;
to prepare for
all that men, and therefore you,

111

expect from us;
to draw fresh hope
as if, this morning, life began;
to struggle against winds and tides,
sustained
by your presence and your promise,
carrying as we do, in us,
men's hopes and all their fears.
Give us breath to live, your breath
that you send from God the Father;
your Spirit, the Breath
that blows where it will;
in gusts or sudden winds
or that light touch
with which you call us to follow.
Breathe on us,
inspire in us,
that prayer which rises from you within us,
calling for you to come in glory,
reaching out to the fullness of God.

Lord, I need your eyes,
give me a living faith.
I need your heart,
a love to withstand any test.
I need the breath of God,
give your hope
to me and all your Church
that the Church today
bear witness to the world,
that the world may know
all Christians,
by their look of joy and serenity,
a warm and generous heart
and the unfailing optimism
that rises

from that secret, everlasting spring
of joyful hope.[1]

[1] Prayer published in L. J. Cardinal Suenens, *A New Pentecost?* London, Collins Fountain, 1977, New York, Seabury Press, 1975. Used by permission.

13

A Farewell Message

If you were to make a spiritual testament, what would you say?

In fact, I've just written a message of this kind to my Archdiocese, and here's the essence of it:

My dear people in God,
My dear co-workers,

A Few Words of Farewell and Gratitude

The time has come for me to leave you as Archbishop of Brussels-Malines and Primate of Belgium. Another Archbishop will shortly take up these two duties: I ask you most earnestly to pray with me that the Lord may guide this choice and give you a pastor according to his heart's desire and your filial expectations.

Since I intend to stay with you in Brussels, I shall continue to carry out at universal level the task, graciously confirmed by the Holy Father, of promoting the Renewal in the Holy Spirit and ecumenical relationships. With the grace of God, I shall devote the best of my strength to this mission, in the hope of serving mankind to the utmost and until my last breath.

When a friend says farewell, his words are charged with a special weight and significance: they have, we may say, the value of a spiritual testament. It is in this spirit, and with an emotion that I need not conceal from you, that I am writing these lines. And also with a keen awareness that I have not always matched up to what the Lord and you yourselves expected of your Bishop during those long, eventful years which we have lived through together. They have been years of transition, of evolution, bringing with them much suffering and tension, but also progress and hopes for the renewal of the Church. As I now commit to the Lord's mercy my shortcomings in the tasks I have fulfilled or leave uncompleted, I am filled with an immense gratitude to him for the life he has given me to live as the pastor of this Archdiocese.

I am also most grateful to you, and especially to those of you who have been my closest collaborators: the priests, the deacons, the religious and nuns, the many committed lay people who have endeavoured with me to fulfil the mission of witnessing, in the heart of the world, to Jesus Christ and his Gospel.

To all my co-workers who have undertaken, with me, the pastoral care of an immense diocese, I express my gratitude. Their living memory abides in me and in my prayers.

My Wish

My wish for all of them is that our ecclesial coresponsibility may increasingly become a fellowship in the Holy Spirit; for to work together, we must first of all live our prayer, pray on the same wave-length, and share a common hope in this unanimous, persevering prayer.

Each time we celebrate the Eucharist, we say to the Lord:

Humbly we beseech you that sharing in this body and blood of Christ we may be gathered by the Holy Spirit into one body.

May this prayer increasingly penetrate and vivify our organizations of coresponsibility.

Christianity and the Discovery of Jesus Christ

This unity in depth is the foundation of all joint action: each of us will have to live it ever more perfectly, so that our human effort may be fertilized by grace, therefore by the efficacy that stems not from our purely human wisdom, but from the power, the creativity and the promptings of the Spirit.

Turning now, with you, towards tomorrow's Church and those Christians who will be continuing our work, this above all is what I want to say to them: My fellow Christians, my brothers, let yourselves be made ever more Christian by the one perfect Christian, Our Lord Jesus Christ.

The quality of our Christianity depends on our faith in him: the depth of our union with him will be the firmest guarantee of the future of his Church. Our Lord does not ask his disciples to be in the majority in this world; he asks them to act as leaven in the dough, to be the salt of the earth, the light on the lampstand (Matt. 5:14).

What is lacking in too many Christians – I mean Christians who, baptized and confirmed in their early years, have reached adulthood without actualizing, through a personal commitment, the sacramental wealth latent in them – is the experience of truly encountering Jesus Christ, of discovering his face, his word, his demands, of forming a permanent and binding existential relationship with him.

Once, as they paused on the wayside, Jesus asked his disciples point-blank, 'Who do you say I am?' We all know Peter's answer.

To each new generation the Master puts the same

direct, vital question. We cannot possibly fall back on generalities and tell him that we recognize him as an inspiring teacher, an example to be followed, a great prophet, or even the greatest prophet of all times. His decisive question penetrates to the heart, like the unerring thrust of a sharp sword, and on our answer depends the authenticity of our Christianity.

For Christianity is not primarily an 'ism', a body of doctrine, a code of life: above all it is a personal encounter with the risen Christ.

The more I advance in years, the more Christ's face becomes luminous to me, and the more I find his presence attentive, warm, discreet, through all the hazards of life. Increasingly, as the days go by, I see him not only as the one who comes to inspire and animate my life, but also as the safe path, truth incarnate, life ever more abundant.

Little by little, I feel him becoming the very breath of my soul; I see him spanning the whole horizon of my life, like a rainbow dominating the landscape. He is everything at once: the past, the present and the future, both on the personal level and the universal.

Christ Yesterday

Jesus Christ is the key-word of God's creation and human history. He embraces all the ages of history and, more particularly, all the hope of Israel: 'The law carried Christ in its womb.' He is the full answer to the expectancy of the patriarchs and the prophets, of Mary. He is God's promise, the seal of the Covenant since the world began.

Looking back on my own life, I know that he illuminated my youth with the radiance of his power, like the sun at dawn. Softly he murmured in my ear the words that determine an existence: 'Come, follow me!' Little

117

by little, I discovered with wonder his intimate presence, like that of a friend, his sacramental action in the heart of the Church, and especially in the eucharistic mystery.

From that time I have known a mounting experience of light, joy, certitude. I have felt that I was constantly discovering and gaining new proof of the stupendous truth of Jesus' words, 'Whoever sees me, sees my Father' (John 14:19). Jesus, the living monstrance of his Father, has opened up new horizons and brought me glimpses of God that no philosophy has ever given me. I would gladly exchange all the treatises on God I have ever read for that single page of the Gospel where Jesus tells the story of the father and his prodigal son. Through the psychology of this father, who eagerly awaits his son's return and greets him with open arms, I apprehend something of the inconceivable love of our Father in heaven.

And this is enough to give me a glimpse of heaven, even in this life. I believe that the greatest truth goes hand in hand with the greatest love. These words sum up my whole creed.

Christ Today

Jesus is also, and forever, the one who wants to fill me completely and to free me from myself, my narrow views, my ignorance, my sinfulness. Deep within my daily struggle against my weakness, and despite my infidelities, he tirelessly pursues his work of redemption and salvation. He loves me with an indefectible love, and this certitude is the rock of my existence.

Jesus came to save me from myself, from sin, death and the powers of evil. All this is meaningless, alas, for those who proclaim that man is self-sufficient, that sin does not exist, that death is followed by everlasting nothingness, and who rate the powers of evil as myths.

Jesus, whose very name means 'Saviour', is not only he who frees me from myself, but he who comes to us as the Saviour of the world.

When Pope John Paul II addressed the crowds in St Peter's Square at the solemn inauguration of his pontificate, he made a poignant appeal to the men of our time:

> Open the frontiers of states to his saving power, open the economic systems and the political systems, the vast realms of culture, civilization and development. Do not be afraid! Christ knows 'what is in man'. He alone knows! So often today man does not know what lies within himself, in the depths of his soul and heart. So often he is uncertain of the meaning of his life on earth. Allow Christ to speak to man. Only He has the words of eternal life.[1]

May the world retain and heed this message!

Christ Tomorrow

Jesus bears within himself my whole past, my present, my future, and therefore all my hope. 'God', says Father Rahner, 'is the absolute future.' It is Jesus who guides me towards that future, towards the ultimate encounter with our Father in heaven. Jesus illuminates the unknown path of tomorrow like the bright beam from our headlights which, piercing through the thick darkness before us, enables us to avoid the obstacles and to make out where we are going. He is our certitude, the aurora borealis shining in the night. *Scio cui credidi* – 'I know in whom I have believed.' He never deceives us: my own death is already immersed in his – indeed, he has paid the price for our salvation – and his resurrection is already the pledge of mine. Henceforth Good Friday, Easter and Pentecost form one triduum: their mystery

119

belongs to me, it is incorporated into my life. In Jesus all suffering becomes a seed of life. In him and through him, I receive the Holy Spirit each day as a beautiful adventure to be lived through. For the Spirit is invention, creation, the unpredictable, youth. He is the supreme antidote against all the hardships of growing old.

The Future of Christianity and the Apostolic Sense of Christians

Christ Jesus not only quickens the Christian's personal life, but also commands us to carry his Name and his Gospel to the whole world.

And here I would like to re-emphasize most earnestly that 'the Church is mission' in every fibre of its being: 'As my Father sent me, so do I send you.'

We have to obey his command to 'go out' to the whole world, to break adrift from our passivity and to make for the high seas. We do not become fully christianized until we are willing to christianize others, from afar or on our own doorstep. We are not fully evangelized unless we, in turn, become evangelizers. Man does not possess Christianity, he is possessed by it. And he retains it only by spreading it around him. What a revolution Christians would bring about if they, who have received Christianity as their birthright, gained a new, keener awareness of the immense spiritual distress of today's world; if they went out to the world and revealed to it through their words and deeds – for the good deed is also a language – that Jesus Christ bears within him its supreme salvation, the ultimate secret of that human brotherhood which men find so difficult to establish among themselves! Oh, how wonderful it would be if so many mute, passive Christians were ready to accept the logic of their faith and to adopt as their own motto St

120

Paul's phrase, 'I believed and therefore I spoke' (2 Cor. 4:13).

The Exhortation 'Evangelii Nuntiandi'

In his Apostolic Exhortation *Evangelii nuntiandi*, Paul VI, summing up the fruits of the discussions of the 1974 Synod of Bishops, has drawn up, with depth and insight, the charter of a Christianity that gives living witness in the heart of the world.

We have to reread that major document, from which I have selected these important passages:

> The Church remains in the world when the Lord of glory returns to the Father. She remains as a sign – simultaneously obscure and luminous – of a new presence of Jesus, of his departure and of his permanent presence. She prolongs and continues him. And it is above all his mission and his condition of being an evangelizer that she is called upon to continue. For the Christian community is never closed in upon itself. The intimate life of this community – the life of listening to the Word.and the Apostles' teaching, charity lived in a fraternal way, the sharing of bread – this intimate life only acquires its full meaning when it becomes a witness, when it evokes admiration and conversion, and when it becomes the preaching and proclamation of the Good News. Thus it is the whole Church that receives the mission to evangelize, and the work of each individual member is important for the whole.

> For the Church, evangelizing means bringing the Good News into all the strata of humanity, and through its influence transforming humanity from within and making it new: 'Now I am making the

121

whole of creation new.' But there is no new humanity if there are not first of all new persons renewed by Baptism and by lives lived according to the Gospel. The purpose of evangelization is therefore precisely this interior change, and if it had to be expressed in one sentence, the best way of stating it would be to say that the Church evangelizes when she seeks to convert, solely through the divine power of the Message she proclaims, both the personal and collective consciences of people, the activities in which they engage, and the lives and concrete milieux which are theirs.

Strata of humanity which are transformed: for the Church it is a question not only of preaching the gospel in ever wider geographic areas or to ever greater numbers of people, but also of affecting and as it were upsetting, through the power of the Gospel, mankind's criteria of judgement, determining values, points of interest, lines of thought, sources of inspiration and models of life, which are in contrast with the Word of God and the plan of salvation.[2]

A New Pentecost

To be worthy of such an ideal, we must be ready to relive, personally, the staggering transformation undergone by the apostles in the Cenacle of Jerusalem on the day of Pentecost. The Holy Spirit covered them with his shadow and his power and utterly transformed them.

Until that moment they had been just frightened disciples of Jesus, running away and hiding without really understanding what the crucial drama of Calvary was all about.

But those same disciples came out of the Upper Room

as apostles of the Lord, faithful unto death to the Master, witnesses to the Resurrection and unafraid of martyrdom. We have to take up the Acts of the Apostles and read them again with new eyes. Then we must ask ourselves, 'Do we or do we not faithfully adhere to this vision of Christianity?'

To contemplate the Church dawning on the morning of Pentecost is also to discover Mary, the Mother of the Church. Here, too, we find her inseparably united to the mysteries of her Son. To those who are afraid of over-estimating the role of Mary – and here I am not speaking of private devotions and revelations which do not belong to the heritage of our faith – I would simply repeat the angel's message to Joseph: 'Do not fear to take Mary home as your wife, for that which is conceived in her is of the Holy Spirit' (Matt. 1:20). The quality of our devotion to Mary is a test of our Christian authenticity.

Towards the Final Stage

As for me, the future is illuminated by the expectation of finally encountering the Lord.

The other day a stranger approached me at the door of the Cathedral and asked me, 'Is death something to fear?' I replied, 'No. We're all on our way to the Father's House, and we're expected there with all those we've known and loved here below. This is the supreme rendezvous. Keep it with a joyful heart!'

The Christians of the primitive Church eagerly looked forward to the Master's glorious return. They were mistaken about the hour and the moment. But they were not mistaken in their keen, intense longing. This Advent is an integral part of every Christian life. As St Theresa of Avila lay dying, she uttered the heartfelt cry, 'At last, Lord, we shall meet!'

Only the Lord knows the hour of the encounter. For

my part, I am content to know that the choice of the moment will be dictated by God's generous, attentive mercy. Beyond death – the paschal passover – the God who waits to greet us is an infinitely loving Father, who goes out to welcome his child with open arms. In him, in the fellowship of the saints and the angels, we will know a joy, tenderness and youth that surpass our boldest dreams.

[1] John Paul II, *Inaugural Homily*, 22 October 1978.
[2] *Evangelii nuntiandi*, nos. 15, 18 and 19 (CTS translation).